GARNIER'S BECKET

GARNIER'S BECKET

translated from the 12th-century
VIE SAINT THOMAS LE MARTYR DE CANTORBIRE

of

GARNIER OF PONT-SAINTE-MAXENCE

by

JANET SHIRLEY

LLANERCH

First published in 1975.

Facsimile reprint 1996,
Llanerch Publishers,
Felinfach.

ISBN 1 86143 023 X

This life
of
Thomas Becket
Archbishop of Canterbury
is
dedicated
with affectionate respect
to his successor
Michael Ramsey

CONTENTS

The above divisions and titles are invented now for convenience in reading; the original text is one continuous whole

ILLUSTRATIONS

MAPS

INTRODUCTION

THIS BOOK is a translation of the *Vie Saint Thomas le Martyr,* a biography of Thomas Becket which was written immediately after Becket's death by a poet called Garnier (or Guernes) of Pont-Sainte-Maxence. It is the oldest known life of Becket written in any vernacular language, and has several claims to our attention. The most obvious one is that it is an important source for the life of its subject, but it is perhaps even more important than that in the light it throws upon the whole of 12th-century society. It constantly makes us aware of the thoughts, hopes and anxieties of the people who lived then, their notions of right and wrong, honour and dishonour, liberty and oppression, and makes us aware too, how startlingly different these can be from the ones that we in our time take for granted.

The *Vie Saint Thomas* also has an important place in the history of literature, both because it stands very early in the development of true biography from saints' lives, and because it is an excellent example of the elegance and skill of 12th-century *trouveurs.* Not only is it useful, it is entertaining.

Date and Reliability

The *Vie Saint Thomas* was written very soon indeed after Thomas Becket was murdered in 1170. Internal evidence is positive on this, but it is also confusing. Garnier says that he began the work 'in the second year after the saint's death' and finished it 'in the fourth year'. Also, in a different passage, he says that he spent four years working on it; and that he had to do it all over twice, as the first version was stolen from him. Different authorities have interpreted these statements differently, but certainly Walberg's point seems conclusive: that the Epilogue dates the completion of the work to the years 1173-75, since Mary, abbess of Barking, and Odo, prior of Canterbury, who are named in it, did not hold these posts before 1173 and after July 1175 respectively.

Garnier, then, wrote near enough in time to the events he relates, to be a useful witness. How far, we may ask, is he otherwise reliable? He claimed total accuracy 'No story as good as this has ever been composed . . . It contains nothing but the exact truth'; where any other writers take a different line, quite simply 'they are wrong'. But then all medieval writers claimed total accuracy. The more fantastic the fable they were presenting, the more careful they were to give it a circumstantial pedigree. 'The original of the following narrative', they would say, 'is kept in a cupboard on the left of the door in the library at So-and-So cathedral, where Master Richard Roe, the respected archdeacon, knows all about it'. Do Garnier's assertions of truthfulness come merely into this category?

Not wholly, no. A claim may be routine practice, and yet true. We can tell from reading his text that Garnier did aim at historical accuracy. He included, for instance, the translations of a number of documents in his text; he had the true mongoose instinct of go-and-find-out, spending over a year at Canterbury checking his evidence, and getting on to excellent terms with Thomas's sisters at Barking and at Canterbury. Often he amplifies or corrects the *Vita Sancti Thomae* of Edward Grim, which he used as his main source. (The complex question of the exact relationship to each other of the Latin *Lives* and the *Vie Saint Thomas* is dealt with in Walberg, pages xxiv-lv and lxv-xcix.) Garnier liked to be precise: he put in the names of places or people where Grim had not done so; where the Latin *Lives* state, in a grave general way, that the palace was plundered, Garnier highlights the passage with a list of the goods stolen—a sapphire, samite, silver and gold, fine jewels which Thomas 'would not show to everyone'. Admittedly this might simply be a case of the artist adding picturesque touches, irrespective of their truth or falsity, but against this charge it can truly be claimed that wherever Garnier can be checked, from documents or from other biographers, he proves to be reliable.

Of course he is not always accurate. Sometimes he copies his sources' error, as when he places the coronation of the Young King too early; or he may present an episode twice over, once from each of two sources, as if it were two different events, as when he makes Thomas suffer the same nightmare twice (pages 96 and 102), although this may perhaps be an attempt at epic repetition. Inevitably everything is presented from the clerkly point of view, with Thomas as the hero and Henry as the villain. In common with the other biographers, Garnier records the fact that Henry had Thomas driven away from Pontigny, and passes over in silence the provocation Thomas had given him. in the sentences of excommunication pronounced so unexpectedly at Vézelay. Unlike some of the other writers, he suppresses or softens the insults which they allege that Thomas shouted at his opponents at Northampton and at Reginald FitzUrse during the final conflict at Canterbury. Garnier's Thomas is a restrained and dignified figure. Whether he was so or not, we cannot say, but this does not invalidate Garnier's historical accuracy. That contemporary writers differed in their presentation of Thomas does not reflect on their honesty or competence, but demonstrates the complexity of the subject with which they dealt.

The Author

All that we know about the author of the *Vie Saint Thomas* is what he tells us himself in this text directly or indirectly. No other works of his are known. His name was Garnier (or Guernes; see note on page 185); he was a clerk in holy orders, and his birthplace was the little town of Pont-Sainte-Maxence. This lay just far enough inside the Ile-de-France to lend justice to Garnier's claim that 'my language is good, for I was born in France', yet near enough to Picardy for an occasional Picardism to creep in. He spent four years almost immediately after Thomas's death in the research for and writing of two versions of his *Vie Saint Thomas.* The first of these was stolen from him; the second is the one translated here.

Much of Garnier's character is revealed by his work. It is clear that he was pushing and persuasive, that he was hard working, skilled in his art and a master of French—although not as proficient in the Latin tongue as he might have been: more than once he misinterprets his sources. This devotion to the cause of Saint Thomas and Holy Church is no more than one would expect from any clerk, but the passionate conviction with which he expresses it has a personal ring. More personal still are the reflections Garnier utters from time to time—as for instance his valiant attempt to reconcile the apparent heartlessness of predestination with the loving nature of a God who 'calls us all, Jew and Gentile, pagan and Christian', to redemption; or his repeated attacks on the savage cruelty of Henry II's forest laws ('killing fine men for the sake of dumb beasts'). His scathing assessment of the brutish peoples over whom Henry II had of necessity to rule by fear, comes no doubt from an outlook peculiar to a class rather than to an individual.

The Epilogue, the short poem of acknowledgments that comes at the end of the *Vie Saint Thomas,* shows Garnier to us most clearly of all. He was a wandering author, one who lived by his art and took what he could get where he could get it in return for his services. We can see him as he rides away from Barking on the horse they so kindly gave him there; he is comfortably provided for, and comfortably aware, too, that he has earned every penny of it.

Genre and Style of the *Vie Saint Thomas*

Garnier's poem consists of some 6,000 lines grouped in five-lined monorhymed stanzas. It is a little difficult to classify—perhaps one might call it an heroic biography. It is essentially an historical work, a true biography, but is written in what often sounds like an epic manner. The line used is the dignified and serious alexandrine; there are several attempts at the epic technique of repetition; the whole poem is a lively, emphatic creation, written not for quiet study but to be enjoyed by a listening audience. The author indeed tells us that he often read parts of it out beside its hero's tomb in the cathedral at Canterbury. It was both a serious work and a tourist attraction.

The author's style is always competent—pathetic or heroic, scornful, lofty or dramatic, whatever was needed, Garnier could supply. He had a wide vocabulary, and excelled in the skills required of his trade in his time—in the elegant use of synonyms, for instance, and in the equally elegant trick of the repetition three or four times of an identical word in differing senses. His dialogue is lively and alert; his creation of character especially convincing.

There is no need to go deeply into the question of the language in which the poem was written; it is a specialised topic, and most thoroughly dealt with by Walberg, on pages cxli-clxv. Briefly, Walberg concludes that the language is principally that of the Ile-de-France, slightly affected by Picard, and by Anglo-Norman.

Some Points of Translation

I have tried to be exact and take no liberties with the text. One that could not be avoided was the substitution of proper nouns for pronouns; in a long passage where the speech or action is tossed from character to character and the modern reader puzzles over which 'he' is speaking to which 'him', it has seemed sensible to insert an occasional 'Thomas' or 'Henry'.

Some of the words I have used need explaining: one such is 'baron'. Garnier often uses it to refer to Thomas, and I have kept the same word in English. It meant more than 'a great lord' or 'one who held estates in barony', although Thomas was those too; it meant essentially any man having authority over others. Thus right to the end of the Middle Ages a woman even of the lower classes would refer to her husband as her 'baron'. It also meant a man of noble character, almost one might say 'our hero'. It is in both these senses that Garnier so often calls Thomas 'the baron'—as being a great man who had, and who deserved to have, great authority.

Another word that was awkward to translate was *dan,* a title of respect deriving from *dominus.* With some hesitation I decided to use 'Sir' for this word. This does well enough when applied to a noble layman such as Richard de Lucy, but does not go so well with the names of clerics. However, it was used for them in Shakespeare's time, and the only other alternative, that of keeping the word *dan,* which exists in Middle English, seemed even more archaic than 'Sir'.

Garnier's principal inaccuracies will be found mentioned in the footnotes. No mention, however, is made of the occasions when he has simply presented events in the light most favourable to Thomas; this is more an attitude of mind than anything else, and to comment on it whenever it is shown would be tedious. Nor will mention always be made of Garnier's divergences from the other sources, as space for footnotes is limited, and the question is fully dealt with by Walberg. Robertson's biography (see below) is very clear and helpful on this.

For similar reasons, the more obvious biblical references have not been noted. Line references given are to Walberg's edition of the text. I have principally used his 1922 edition, with some help from that by Hippeau.

Manuscripts of the *Vie Saint Thomas*

Six manuscripts, not all complete, were known to Walberg; he describes them fully on pages cxi-cxxxv of his edition. They are all Anglo-Norman, and none are older than the 13th century. The three oldest, early 13th-century, are: Wolfenbüttel, the duke of Brunswick's library, 34.6; British Museum, Harley 270; and Bibliothèque Nationale, fonds français 13513. This is the only one to contain the Epilogue. Welbeck Abbey ICI is late 13th- or early 14th-century. Phillipps Collection 8113 and British Museum Cotton Domitian XI are both 14th century. Walberg also mentions a fragment in the Bodleian. Another fragment has been found since his edition was published, and is referred to by Professor M. D. Legge on page 249 of her *Anglo-Norman Literature.*

Editions of the Text

The earliest edition of the *Vie Saint Thomas* was that of the incomplete 13th-century Wolfenbüttel manuscript by I. Bekker in the *Transactions of the Berlin Academy,* 1838. He completed it in 1844 from the 13th-century British Museum manuscript.

Le Roux de Lincy published a description and synopsis of B.N. fonds français 13513, together with long extracts, in the *Bibliothèque de l'Ecole des Chartes,* 4, 1842-43, pages 208-241.

In 1859 a charming but now rare edition of this same manuscript was published by C. Hippeau.

An edition of the *Vie Saint Thomas* was to have been included in the Rolls Series, *Materials for the Life of Thomas Becket,* but this plan did not come to anything.

The authoritative edition of the text is that published in Lund, Sweden, and jointly with the O.U.P., by Emmanuel Walberg, in 1922. This is based on a comparison of all the manuscripts and considers every aspect of the text in the most thorough detail. (This is the edition on which my translation is chiefly based.) This edition is also published, with a shortened critical apparatus, in the series *Classiques Français du Moyen Age.*

Bibliography

The following is a list of books used, and referred to in the footnotes. Some that readers may find particularly interesting are marked with an asterisk; but those who would like to know more about Thomas Becket and his times are strongly recommended to begin by reading the recent biography by David Knowles (*Thomas Becket*, A. and C. Black, 1970). Besides being invaluable in itself, this contains on pages 172-178 a clear survey of medieval writings on St. Thomas and a most helpful review of 19th- and 20th-century work. More recent still is W. L. Warren's *Henry II.*

Books used include:—

Tancred Borenius, *St. Thomas Becket in Art* (Methuen, 1932). Interesting on the growth of the saint's legend.

The Dictionary of National Biography (O.U.P., 1917–), abbreviated *D.N.B.*

William Dugdale, *Monasticon Anglicanum* (London, 1846).

English Historical Documents, ed. Douglas and Greenaway (Eyre and Spottiswood, 1959), vol. 2, abbreviated *E.H.D.*

*Gilbert Foliot, *Letters and Charters*, ed. Brooke and Morey (C.U.P., 1967).

Robert Furley, *A History of the Weald of Kent* (Ashford and London, 1871).

Geoffrey of Monmouth, *History of the Kings of Britain*, tr. L. Thorpe (Penguin Classics, 1966).

Louis Halphen, 'Les entrevues des rois Louis VII et Henri II durant l'exil de Thomas Becket en France' in *Mélanges d'histoire offerts à M. Charles Bémont* (Paris, 1913).

Louis Halphen, 'Les biographes de Thomas Becket' in *Revue historique*, cii (1909), 35-45.

Honorius of Autun, Scala dei minor in J.-P. Migne, *Patrologiae Cursus Completus*, Series Secunda, clxxii (Paris, 1854).

*David Knowles, *Archbishop Thomas Becket, a character study*, in *Proceedings of the British Academy*, vol. xxxv, and in *Historian and Character* (C.U.P., 1963).

*David Knowles, *The Episcopal Colleagues of Thomas Becket* (C.U.P., 1951), abbreviated *E.C.*

*David Knowles, *Thomas Becket* (A. and C. Black, 1970).

Beatrice A. Lees, *Records of the Templars in England in the Twelfth century: The Inquest of 1185* (O.U.P., 1935).

*M. Dominica Legge, *Anglo-Norman Literature and its Background* (Clarendon Press, 1963).

Le Roux de Lincy, 'La vie et la mort de Saint Thomas de Cantorbéry, par Garnier de Pont-Sainte-Maxence' in the *Bibliothèque de l'Ecole des Chartes* 1842-43, iv., 208-241.

Materials for the Life of Thomas Becket, ed. J. C. Robertson, Rolls Series 67 (London, 1875), abbreviated *Materials.*

*A. M. Morey and C. L. N. Brooke, *Gilbert Foliot and his Letters* (C.U.P., 1965).

*Kate Norgate, *England under the Angevin Kings* (London, 1887.

Pipe Rolls for 21 Henry II, 1174-75, xxii (London, 1897).

F. Pollock and F. W. Maitland, *The History of English Law before the Time of Edward I* (C.U.P., 1911).

*J. C. Robertson, *Becket, archbishop of Canterbury* (London, 1859). Readable as well as scholarly, and one of the few writers on Becket who knows Garnier's text.

J. H. Ramsay, *The Angevin Empire* (London, 1903).

J. H. Round, *Feudal England* (London, 1895); also, *Geoffrey de Mandeville* (London, 1892): and *The Commune of London* (London, 1899). Especially interesting for the world and political situation in which Becket grew up.

*A. Saltman, *Theobald, Archbishop of Canterbury* (London, 1956).

Select Charters, ed. Stubbs and Davis (O.U.P., 1957).

Thomas Saga Erkibyskups, ed. Magnusson, Rolls Series 65 (London, 1875).

*William Urry, *Canterbury under the Angevin Kings* (London, 1967).

William Urry, 'The Visions of Master Feramin' in the *39th Annual Report of the Friends of Canterbury Cathedral* (1966); and his 'Two notes on Guernes de Pont-Sainte-Maxence' in *Archaeologia Cantiana,* lxvi, 92-95.

The Victorian County History of Kent, ed. W. Page (London, 1908 and 1926), abbreviated *V.C.H.*

ACKNOWLEDGMENTS

THE DRAWINGS by Ruth Stiven are based on medieval originals. Those on pages 20 and 55 are taken from the early 14th-century *Queen Mary's Psalter,* by courtesy of the trustees of the British Museum. The next five are based on drawings in a mid-13th-century manuscript published by Paul Meyer, S.A.T.F., 1885, and now forming part of the Mansell Collection, London. The picture of Thomas's death on page 155 is drawn from the earliest known representation of the murder, late 12th-century, in B.M. Harl. 5102, also by courtesy of the trustees of the British Museum. The picture on page 164 showing St. Thomas's tomb, and the use of the miraculous water for healing, is based on an early 13th-century window in the cathedral at Canterbury and appears by permission of the Dean and Chapter and of Lund, Humphries Ltd. The maps were drawn by Helen Buchanan and Ian Hamilton.

I would like to record here my gratitude to those who have helped me in making this translation, including especially Dr. A. B. Emden, Dr. William Urry, Professor M. Dominica Legge, David Shirley, Dr. R. B. Barlow, and Mrs. P. M. Matarasso.

York
Beverley
Hull
Humber
Lincoln
Hermitage
Haverholme Priory
Boston
Stoke-on-Trent
Grantham
Sempringham Priory
Greetham
afford
Lynn
Gretton
Isle of Ely
Ely
Warwick
Northampton
Cambridge
Bedford
Chicksands Priory
Colchester
Gloucester
Woodstock
Thames
Oxford
Harrow
LONDON
Barking
Southwark
Merton
Rochester
Canterbury
Sandwich
Dover
Old Sarum
Clarendon
Salisbury
Winchester
Hythe
Rye
Romney
Winchelsea
Southampton
Hastings
Chichester
Pevensey
Portsmouth

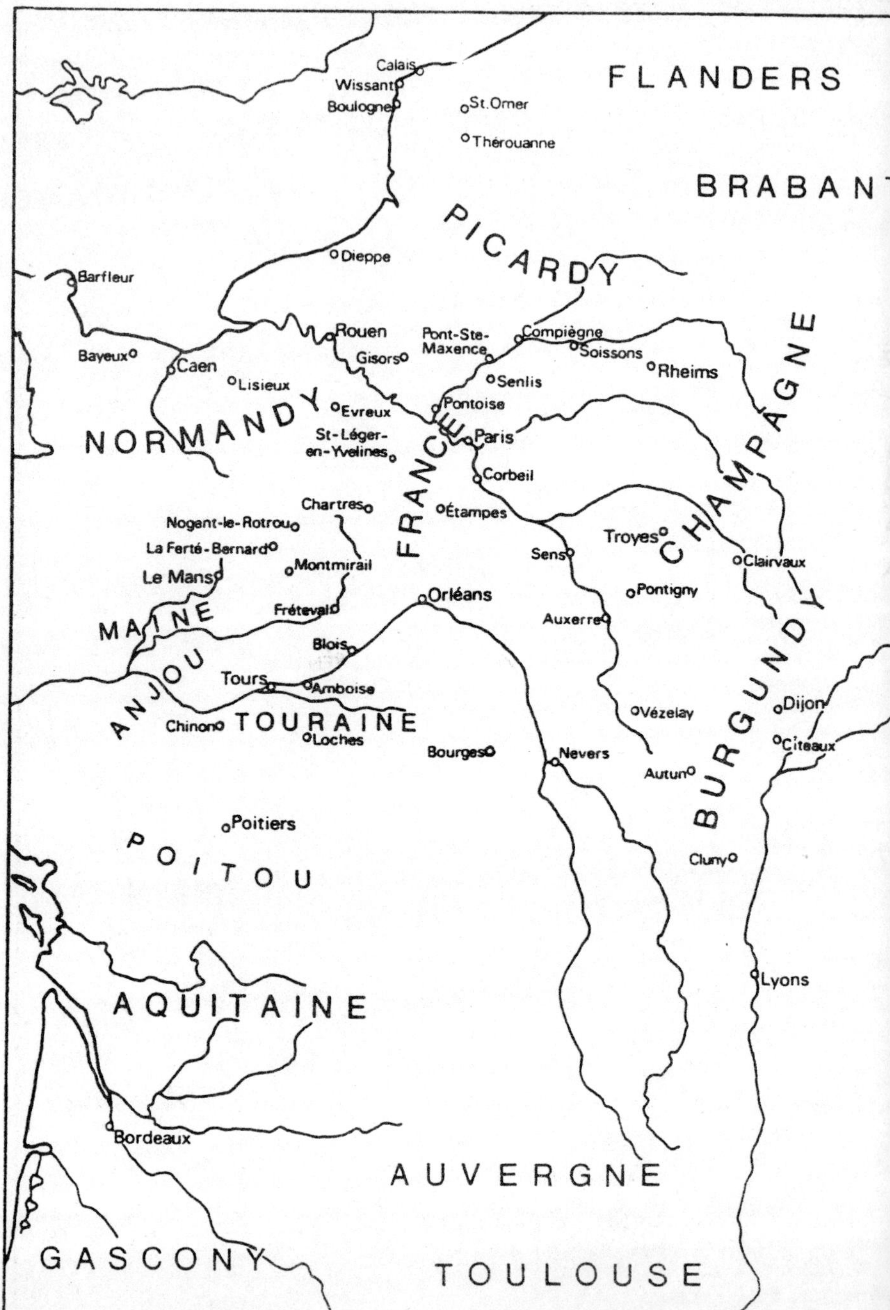

FLANDERS
BRABANT
Calais
Wissant
Boulogne
St.Omer
Thérouanne
PICARDY
Dieppe
Barfleur
Rouen
Pont-Ste-Maxence
Compiègne
Soissons
Rheims
CHAMPAGNE
Bayeux
Caen
Gisors
Senlis
Lisieux
Evreux
Pontoise
NORMANDY
St-Léger-en-Yvelines
Paris
FRANCE
Corbeil
Chartres
Étampes
Nogant-le-Rotrou
La Ferté-Bernard
Troyes
Sens
Clairvaux
Le Mans
Montmirail
Orléans
Pontigny
Fréteval
MAINE
Auxerre
Blois
BURGUNDY
Tours
Amboise
ANJOU
Vézelay
Dijon
Chinon
TOURAINE
Loches
Bourges
Nevers
Cîteaux
Autun
Poitiers
POITOU
Cluny
Lyons
AQUITAINE
Bordeaux
AUVERGNE
GASCONY
TOULOUSE

Salisbury
Winchester
Southampton
Portsmouth
Chichester
Pevensey
Hastings
Winchelsea
Rye
Romney
Hythe
Saltwood
Dover
Charing
Harbledown
CANTERBURY
Eastry
Sandwich
Calais
Gravelines
Marck
Wissant
Boulogne
St. Omer
Clairmarais
Thérouanne
Amiens
Dieppe
Barfleur
Harfleur
Rouen
Bur
Bayeux
Caen

PROLOGUE

A MAN may be a doctor, yet sometimes fail to cure his patients; or a clerk, but be incapable of singing mass as he should–or a writer, and yet find that the right phrases escape him. Perhaps a man will select utter rubbish, thinking it perfection; or someone may plume himself on being superior to everyone else, when in fact he is just the opposite. Anyone who hopes to create any kind of poem, any discourse or treatise, must take endless pains over his writing, and then no one will laugh at him or pick up some trivial fault in his work which may make the whole thing ridiculous. Good sense should be clearly expressed, evil left out; thus the good will prove helpful and no one will be harmed.

11 And so I have embarked on the task I am hoping to complete if Christ, lord of us all, allows it: a description of the life of Saint Thomas of Canterbury, who died a martyr for his mother church, and who is now, incontrovertibly, a most mighty saint in heaven.[1]

17 Everyone knows that people in this world are of very differing characters and lives. Many are poor, some rich; some love good sense, a great many more love foolishness; some love God, most follow the guidance of Satan. My lords, for the love of God and for your own salvation, turn away from empty things, pay attention to my words! None of you is incapable of understanding reason. Take no notice, no notice whatever, of that traitor's suggestions, for what use is a profit that will bring you to damnation? Honour God, holy church, and the clergy; shelter the poor and feed and clothe them; pay your tithes on everything honestly; guard yourself from every kind of criminal sin; and I tell you truly, you shall possess the Lord God.

31 Grievously, most grievously, was holy church at first oppressed, and by the king's deliberate purpose most unjustly persecuted. Thanks be to God, who has now looked on her again! She will be restored, by the man who of his own will suffered the death blow for her. It was the king's constant habit to do injustice and violence to clerks; any who were found doing wrong were forced by him to submit to laymen's judgment;[2] they could not avoid it. This Thomas supported them; he was their only strength; he fought for them to the death. If clerks do wrong, let God avenge it—they are your superiors, it is not for you to judge them. Then they may commit fresh sins, sins so horrible that they lose their orders, but you cannot impose anything more on them. If after that they are caught doing wrong, then you may punish them. Saint Thomas conceded this, though neither civil nor canon law authorise it, in order to restrain the king from any angry or violent outbreak, but none of the saints allow it, nor do I grant it. I do not see how a bishop can take away from a clerk the sacrament he has received from the King of Heaven. At Elijah's prayer, God made rain fall on the earth, which was almost perishing of want, for no drop had fallen for 42 months; but the prophet would never have been able to send this rain back again afterwards. You can see clearly how evil the king's intention was. He has no right to forbid anything to church or clerk, nor to take anything of theirs, but ought to add to them—and he takes to himself the church's crown and her laws! May God amend it, the One in Three!

61 It is obvious that Saint Thomas was right in fighting as he did for the oppressed clergy; he did it for the love of God as he should have done, and God, who deceives no one, has repaid it to him. No one can contradict this, for everyone can see it. The whole world runs to him, bishops and abbots, gentle and simple, fief-holding princes —and no one sends for them, they go of their own accord. People who have not been there, hurry to go; even little children are carried there in their cradles. There, the dumb speak, the deaf can hear, many recover from leprosy, many from dropsy, cripples stand up straight, the dead live again, light returns to the blind. Saint Thomas is quick to help anyone who earnestly and sincerely begs him to do so. One remarkable thing we observe, which is proved to be quite genuine, is that the water in which his bloodstained clothes were washed heals both internal and external diseases. It has cured a thousand, either by drinking or by being washed with it, and has brought several dead back to life.

81 Kings, earls and dukes very rarely become saints. God withholds a great deal from them, for they are not willing to serve him. Greed often makes them leave what is right; they do nothing but what they please, make laws to suit themselves, and are not afraid of death. God does not choose kings, he does not call or accept them, nor dukes, nor other great persons—it is the man who fears God and lives rightly, be he high born or low, whom God exalts and makes much of, if he applies himself to serving him. Saul, the first king of the Jews, was born of common people; truly, God chose him. He rode to war against God's enemies for a long time, until at last he disobeyed God's command, and all because of greed; God took vengeance for it. In his place God chose David the son of Jesse, a red-complexioned shepherd boy, born of a poor family; the prophet anointed him and he was king all his life, noble, learned, and of great authority; he made amends humbly when he had done wrong. What a fool is the man who insists on lying long in his sin! Let him beg God for mercy, lest he fall asleep in it. It is only too easy to wreck one's life by sin, and many are so overwhelmed at the moment of death that they cannot open their mouths or speak to a priest. God loves humble men, and the poor too, for they live by their own labour, they exist in constant suffering; and they love holy church and the clergy and the poor; they pay their proper tithes and live clean lives—God will exalt such men throughout eternity. Peter and Andrew, too, they were brothers, fishermen working with boats and nets, when God called them from this poor toil; later they were crucified and died for his love; they are apostles in heaven and most glorious lords.

116 And so I have begun to compose this discourse for you about the martyr Saint Thomas, that glorious lord to whom all men flock at the holy house of the blessed Trinity,[3] where he suffered his passion because he supported truth and reason.

Oh you unhappy man, why did you kill this most holy archbishop? His death gained you nothing, and he had done no wrong; what a foul error you made. Repent, repent quickly! Can you wish to be destroyed? You have, and will have, amends to make, even if you could live for ever. Do you want to lose your soul, for the sake of the filthy body, which will be dead and gone in a moment, before you can be aware of it? The glory of this world is no fief, no inheritance; like it or not you must leave it all behind. Castles and strongholds will not guard you against God. The merciful and true God held Saint Thomas very dear. He was killed in a beautiful place, in a holy church, killed by barons and vassal knights; there they lost all their worth; can they make good their loss? Yes, if they want to, they can be reconciled to God. No sinner can commit any sin, however foul, but the moment he repents and turns wholly away from it, God forgives and strengthens him. It was for this that God suffered death for sinners' sakes; when they come to him, he brings them safe to harbour.

141 If you would like to listen to the life of the holy martyr, you may hear it now, fully treated by me. I want to be accurate, to say nothing that is not true, and have spent almost four years working on it; I know how to bear the burden of crossing out and writing in again. At first I worked by hearsay, and made many mistakes; then I went to Canterbury and heard the truth—I collected the truth from Saint Thomas's friends and from those who had served him since childhood. I worked hard, taking out and putting in. This first version, however, was stolen from me by scribes before I had corrected and finished it, before I had balanced the bitter and the sweet or shortened the passages that were too long. It is sometimes incorrect and is not complete, but it does contain the major part of the truth, and many rich men have bought it—although those who stole it are much to be blamed. However, I have finished and perfected this one in every way. I hear frequent inaccuracies in all the other narratives that have been written about the martyr, whether by clerks or laymen, monks or a lady;[4] they are neither accurate nor complete. But here you can listen to the truth, the complete truth; I shall not stray from the truth, not if I were to die for it.

CHAPTER ONE

Early Career

166 SAINT THOMAS the archbishop, of whom you hear me speak, was begotten in London, descended from and brought up among the lords of that city. His father's name was Gilbert Becket and his mother's Matilda; he was born of decent people.[1] When his mother first conceived him, she dreamed that the water of the Thames entered her womb, and a learned man to whom she told this explained it, saying, 'Your heir shall rule over many people'. I think that she carried living water in her womb! Another beautiful dream God sent her was that she thought she went to Holy Trinity, and when she tried to go through the door her belly swelled up so big that she could not get through; indeed, I think that all Sion cannot contain his goodness! Another time she dreamed that when she was to have the child, the 12 great stars of heaven fell down into her lap—there is deep meaning here, for all the 12 tribes bow to him and he will be one of the 12 men who will judge them.[2] After she had had the child, she dreamed again, this time that it was lying uncovered in its cradle; she was very upset about this and asked the nurse to cover the baby up—the nurse answered that the child was very well covered up under a big silken coverlet,[3] folded over. (The coverlet was red.) They both got up and hurried urgently to unfold the coverlet, but the room was too small. They went into the house, but it was too small too, so they went out into the street, and that was not big enough. They went to Smithfield,[4] and still Smithfield was much smaller than the coverlet; then they heard a voice coming down to them, saying that all England would not be able to contain the greatness of this coverlet—we see that this means that the saint's blood must spread all over the world. He was sent to school quite young, and then set to grammar when he had done the psalter; then to the arts, after he had done some singing. He studied hard and took pains, but did not continue long at the schools.[5]

206 Richer de Laigle[6] often used to put up at Thomas's father's house, and Thomas used to go to the woods and the river with him. They were companions for at least six months, as I have heard. It was at this period that Thomas began to be very fond of hawks and hounds. One day the boy went along the river with Richer de Laigle; he wanted to learn about hawks' behaviour and leashes. They came to a broad dyke where there was no bridge or road across, nothing but a plank by which people walked over. The baron went ahead and the boy followed him. The knight crossed over; Thomas, wrapped in a hooded cloak, came next, but his horse stumbled and both horse and rider fell into the dyke. Thomas left the saddle and was carried downstream. There was a mill near the plank which was working, going full tilt; Thomas was carried down, and just as he must have fallen head first into the wheel, the miller finished his work and shut off the flow. So God saved the child from death at this time, for he wanted to preserve him in order to accomplish great good through him. God allows some men to flourish because they are to be the means of accomplishing great harm; others, on the contrary, are to enable much good to be done.

230 He was 21 or more years old, it is said, when he left the university;[7] most unfortunately his resources came to an end, he had very little support, for his parents were shipwrecked in a whirlpool from which they could never afterwards rise to their proper harbour again. His father had once been a very rich man, and his mother a beautiful woman in face and figure. They came of a good family and had done very well, but fire had severely damaged and destroyed them; they suffered so often from fire that they were all but ruined. Thomas went to a relation of his, an important Londoner called Osbern Huit-Deniers,[8] who at once gave him employment; he was a man very well known, both among French and Englishmen. Thomas was his secretary for either two years or three, I do not know which. He now began to be both wise and courteous.

Clerk to Theobald

246 Thomas was very busy, upstream, downstream, so much so that he joined the household of the Archbishop.[9] He did this by means of a marshal of the Archbishop's, who used to stay at Thomas's father's house. Well dressed and well mounted he went to him, with the King of Heaven as his helper.[10]

251 Thomas was clever, and God increased him greatly in wisdom and in powers of thought. He was alert day and night and took pains to serve his lord in all that he could and was a particularly frequent attender at council meetings; the archbishop often summoned him to them. Roger of Pont l'Evêque[11] was jealous of him, and whenever he could he got him sent away, either himself or by means of others. He often used to refer to him as 'Baille-Hache's clerk' (that was the name of the man who had brought him to court).[12] But Thomas was no fool, and got the better of him. Archbishop Theobald took him to Rome, and Thomas often went there afterwards as his messenger. There or elsewhere, he served him so satisfactorily that the Archbishop kept him near his own person and took him into his entire confidence.

266 William, Archbishop of York, died.[13] Archbishop Theobald, who was very distressed at this, obtained the appointment for his archdeacon, Roger of Pont l'Evêque, and consecrated him to the post; he gave the archdeaconry to Thomas, his clerk. He got him made provost of Beverley,[14] and gave him rents and churches in various places, for he had never found anyone whose work pleased him so much. God, who inspired him, gave him success, and he applied himself constantly to honour, wisdom and goodness. He loved hounds and hawks and secular amusements; he was noble and open-handed and had a quick, clear brain; but he did not refuse, if anyone wanted to give him anything, as those do who are able to help or hinder and who want to make their way in the world by means of their wealth.

Chancellor

281 Archbishop Theobald did not forget him: he introduced Thomas into the employment of King Henry II,[15] who at once made him chancellor.[16] So his honours and his riches kept increasing, but he never neglected the king's service. He took pleasure in working for him in everything that he could, and was entirely his, in thought and in deed. Whatever he happened to possess—silver, pence, gold, clothes, horses—he gave to the knights. He was deeply humble at heart, yet arrogant in appearance; he was humble with poor people, proud-looking with the mighty, a lamb inwardly but outwardly a leopard. Early or late, he never delayed in serving and pleasing the king. But whatever he was outwardly, there was not a scrap of falsity in him: he kept all his inmost self for God. Perhaps he may have been proud and given to vanities, as far as worldly cares go and in outward appearance, yet he was chaste in body and healthy in soul. Although he was fully occupied in the king's service, yet as much as he could be, he was holy church's right hand. At this time King Henry II, lord of England, was in Staffordshire; he was in love with a lady, the most elegant in all the empire, as I have heard, Avice of Stafford. But she could see that the king's affection was already dwindling, his passion was beginning to cool, and this grieved her, as she loved him dearly. Thomas the Chancellor was then at Stoke-on-Trent, and this lady often sent messengers to him; the man in whose house he was staying (a light-minded fellow) thought this suspicious. (It was Vivian the clerk with whom he was staying.[17]). One night when Thomas's bed was all carefully made, with a silken cover and expensive fine sheets, this man thought that he was in bed with the lady; he was sure that she had come there. When he supposed that the baron was asleep and had had all his enjoyment of the lady, he took a lantern, wanting to know for certain whether Thomas was betraying the king, and went to the place where the bed was. He found it empty, and was astonished. None of the sheets had been disturbed; it was just as it had been arranged late that evening. Then he imagined that Thomas had gone to the lady, and he held the candle up higher to make sure–there lay wise Thomas on the floor beside the bed. He had a cloak over him, partly covering him, leaving his legs and feet bare. He had worn himself out with praying and had lain down on the floor exhausted and was now fast asleep, because he had watched so long. The more Thomas climbed in the secular world, the humbler he was at heart, whatever he appeared to be. Many times and in many places he did wrong on the king's behalf, but he used to make amends privately to God at night; and that is why God has built so greatly upon this good foundation. No member of his household, clerk or companion, chamberlain or servant, seneschal or serving lad, ever had grounds for suggesting that Saint Thomas was ever guilty of this kind of offence.

341 Thomas was a magnificent clerk and lived in great splendour; Henry the rich king who owns so much of the world did not live in greater–this is no exaggeration. You won't find this year a cleverer man than he was. And he endured much labour and effort in order to serve the king and maintained a big retinue of vassal knights on whom he lavished gifts and provisions, and supported mercenaries, archers and soldiers as well. He led them out of the right way, and sinned grievously, and did great harm to the king's enemies. Castles, mottes and strongholds fell to his assault, burghs and towns were burned, cities attacked; he would sit his warhorse, armed in his strong hauberk, often until he was exhausted. (He wore the hauberk to protect him from arrowshot.) He was in Gascony for a long time, to make war; and compelled the Gascons to surrender some of their castles. In Normandy too he was of great use to his lord; I myself saw him several times riding against the French; his trumpets did much to further the king's cause.[18]

361 This world is evil, you can see it plainly. The more a man has, the less he thinks about knowledge; the more his worldly powers increase, the less use he will be to God, for he then forgets God and neglects him–he wants to embrace the world, and it seeks to possess him. The devil, moreover, never ceases to spy upon the Christian, hoping to entrap him, and the better a man, the more honourable and charitable, he sees him to be, the harder he exerts himself to make him sin, so that he may pull him down with him into hell. This Thomas that I am speaking of, who was then so powerful, never used to act wrongly before he became Chancellor; he was straightforward with everyone, great or small. Now he became very enterprising on his lord's behalf, exerting himself in everything to do what would please him. The Chancellor served the king to the latter's complete satisfaction, and whatever he did Henry approved. He was in his closest confidence, working for his purposes; nothing was concealed from him. There was no-one at that time whom the king loved more. He even put him in charge of Henry, his eldest son,[19] and ordered him to receive all the barons' homage; if there was one of them in the whole kingdom rash or bold enough to refuse, Thomas was commanded to lay siege to him at once. No one could outwit Thomas in anything. If ever the king complained about any wealthy knight, or earl, or baron on whom he wanted vengeance, he never found the Chancellor trying to put in a good word for the man–'Has he behaved so badly towards you?' he said; 'Indeed, it was foolhardy of him even to let it cross his mind. He is a rich man, or very powerful, or has done you much service; he ought to be corrected. It is time he suffered so that you may know the truth of the matter.'[20]

396 When Archbishop Theobald died, the king gave this post to the Chancellor, who was much in his confidence, for he knew of no clerk in the kingdom of comparable excellence and supposed that he would obey all his,

Henry's, inclinations. King Henry was then in Normandy, and so was Thomas, seeking renown and glory; he had the best knights of the country with him and was making war upon Louis, king of France.[21] He was very active in the king's service. There was not a man in the whole kingdom, howevers proud or mighty, who could hurt Thomas, or help him. Whoever came to the king, whatever it was he wanted, was sent straight back to the Chancellor; whatever he did or undid, the king invariably confirmed. He had all England and all Normandy in his control, and other lands too, and the king approved everything he did. He always took a considerable force of knights about with him, and was often of great assistance to the king in his war. There was not a more generous supplier of food in all the land; his establishment was always thronged with barons and knights–harlots and adulterers!–eating and drinking. His house very often emptied the king's, so much so that the king began to be angry about it. Whilst he was archdeacon, provost and Chancellor, Thomas loved orphans, widows, and poor people; he did not have a servant or almoner to set them in order but always gave them food at once and was happy to do so. And the holier the day the more lavish he was to them.

The king now sent Thomas to England, entrusting to him the burden of all his business: he promoted him greatly over this, for he knew him thoroughly, from head to foot, and wanted to retain his friendship in everything.

Choice of a New Archbishop

431 Then the king sent to Holy Trinity three bishops[22] who knew a good deal about his plans, and Richard de Lucy,[23] a very wise baron. They went into the chapter house with the monks,[24] and Richard de Lucy spoke for them all:

'King Henry', he said, 'whom we hold as our lord, has sent to the monastery and to the prior[25] by us: this church has for a long time been without a shepherd; the king now wishes that you should have a father and ruler, but it must be one who will be to your profit and to his honour.'

'God send us', they said, 'a shepherd to his liking who will be able to defend holy church and ourselves. Blessed be the king for allowing us to choose a shepherd for the church!'

'He does not want to take away your rights from you', the bishops said, 'but you must think very carefully, so that you elect a man who will, especially, be useful to you with regard to the king. You must be well aware that if you elect anyone against his will, your church may thereby fall into great loss. You would never have peace or his friendship; you would be forever in schism and discord. But you have no need to make him angry–if you could manage to elect someone whom he loves dearly, then you would be well out of all your difficulties'.

456 The monks discussed this together in council. They called the bishop of Chichester to them; nor did they exclude the bishop of Exeter, and Richard, who held fief and inheritance of them, and they asked them to advise the church of Holy Trinity. They recommended what they thought was the best course, and they so pressed and guided the assembly's opinion that they all consented, old and young, to elect Thomas to this post. The barons agreed to this decision. They were sure that the king would give his assent; no one could choose a more honourable clerk, nor one who could better advance the interests of their church, nor one who was on better terms with the king; if they did what would please him, the church might well benefit very greatly in future.

471 The monks had now definitely consented to this decision, and the barons went to London, where they called together all the barons of the whole country; there were many bishops and abbots present, and the prior of Holy Trinity was there as well. There they elected Thomas and took him for their protector without objection from anyone, learned or lay, except the bishop of London.[26] He disliked the proposal and said that Thomas had persecuted holy church and it would be very wrong indeed that he should have this appointment. Thomas himself spoke against the proposal, opposing them all: he did not deserve, he said, to wear so noble a habit, he had destroyed holy church and despised her laws and always persecuted her; they had been wrong to elect him. He begged with tears for respite and delay.

486 'No, my son', said the bishop of Winchester,[27] 'you must accept. If you have done wrong in secular work, then serve the Lord of Heaven all the better and more eagerly. You have been a wolf to the sheep, now be their pastor and priest. You must and shall change from Saul the persecutor to Paul'. Then with great joy they elevated him to the archbishopric, for the whole body of clergy had chosen and called him. The king had meanwhile sent letters to the judges and the clergy—but they had not disclosed them—ordering delay;[28] that is why they hurried over the matter. I do not know why the king wanted to draw back so soon; he realised, I believe, that his affair was altered—he would not be able to do as he liked with him any more; Thomas would not let him injure the rights of holy church. But no one can hinder what God has willed. Or it may have been that the king saw that Thomas had served him loyally and well in everything, and that he would never find anyone else who would serve him so well; he now regretted that Thomas had left his employment. None the less, they presented him to King Henry's son. (The king had already given him the realm so that whatever might happen to him, he should be secure; he had received homage and oaths of loyalty from everyone.) In his letter to the judges, the king had said that he confirmed whatever arrangements they should make. So they presented this election to the child and to those whom the king had empowered, and these gave their assent and confirmation. The bishop of Winchester, who was a very intelligent man, wanted to be sure that no complaint could ever be raised against them, and he addressed the child and the barons:

517 'My lords', he said, 'listen to me for a moment. This man has been the king's administrator and his close friend; we have elected him and you have confirmed this.

Now we want you to acknowledge him to be quit of any claims. He has been administrator and judge of the country; he has had all the king's rents at his disposal. His church requires that he be declared quit and free from any claim in respect of all accounts, all obligation, everything, so that whatever may occur in the future, she shall not be the loser by it'. The royal judges (to whom the king had said that he confirmed any decision they might make) and the king's son together with them, declared him free of liability for accounts or for any other matter, and they delivered him to the clergy. Then with great joy they raised him to the archbishopric.

Thomas's Consecration

531 Not long after this they took him with much rejoicing to Canterbury where he was most honourably welcomed, and consecrated.[29] But he did not immediately change his style of dress; he wanted his clothing to hide what was deep in his heart. The lords often grumbled about this among themselves—that he had entered the choir with his tunic down to his feet—they did not know what God had built in his heart. Someone who knew him well, rebuked him for this and told him about a dream that a monk had had; God had appeared to the monk and said, as he lay asleep, 'Go quickly to the Chancellor, tell him that I command him to put on monastic dress; he must not delay. If he does not do this, I shall always oppose him, and evil will come to him all his life long'. The Archbishop gave a laugh when he heard this, and told the man something of what he had in mind; but only to God did he open his whole heart, to God who had called and chosen him before he was born. For he was now utterly transformed from his previous self; as soon as he undertook this high office he abandoned evil ways and all secular occupation. He ruled both the clergy and holy church sternly, holding the sword of justice ever ready to strike; neither fear nor great love of gain could affect him. All that he ought to love, he supported and held dear; all that he ought to hate, he abandoned and kept far from him. He never even came near doing anything for the king against God. He clothed the poor and fed them and looked after them; he took pains to serve the Lord God in everything that he could.

561 The monks said to him that since he was their master, their leader, their father, he ought to be their abbot; that since he was abbot, he ought to live and dress as one. He ought to be reborn to that to which he was called; divine honour rejects earthly clothing. The regular canons could not bear that a bishop or archbishop should wear monastic dress—a monk, like a dead man, is given a black cuirass;[30] that dress is not proper for a prelate. These had a good deal of evidence on their side. The clerks who were with him said to him, on the other hand, that if he had been a monk and in that condition, he would have left that life and the monastic order. Since he lived with clerks, he would wear the common dress; he would not hold episcopal power as a monk.

576 Thus he was attacked from three quarters with this kind of reasoning; but he took advice from an excellent man, the prior of Kenilworth,[31] who had clothes made for him. He left off secular dress and wore that of the regulars; he was a canon outwardly but was burdened inwardly. He did not want to display too much of the religious externally, but wanted to wear the two orders both at once on the one body; he wore the cowl underneath his other clothes, that being the order he wanted to conceal, with the sleeves and skirts shortened. Next to his skin, he wore a hair shirt, to distress his body more. He did not want on any account to fail to take monkhood upon him, either because of the vision God had had told to him, or because no one has ever prospered who sought to embrace that honour as a secular. For there were two men whom God flung wretchedly down from it: Stigand[32] was deposed from his see by the Pope and died miserably in prison; and God caused Aelfsige[33] to lose his way in the Mount Jove mountains; he had his mare cut open and plunged his feet in, but died of cold inside the animal, he could not contrive to get warm.

The Pallium Obtained

596 Thomas then sent for the abbot of Evesham, Sir Adam of Senlis,[34] an excellent and famous man, and ordered him to go to fetch his pallium.[35] Two good clerks and a monk[36] went with him and they found Pope Alexander[37] at Montpellier. They were scholarly men, competent in the arts, in canon and in civil law; each of the three spoke very well and like educated men. Alexander the Pope listened attentively to them, I am sure, but he did not grant them the pallium. They approached the cardinals more than once about the question, and the cardinals constantly wanted to know what they had brought to the Pope and to themselves, for they had been forced to flee from Rome and had not got a penny of their incomes. The messengers at once replied that they had come there from a distant land, that they had spent almost all that they had brought with them; they wanted to receive the pallium in a straightforward and honourable way; never should anyone suppose them to be simonists. They could get no more, however much they kept asking. Then when the abbot perceived a good occasion for him to speak, and saw the cardinals standing round the Pope, he began to set forth his request most excellently–but he avoided making any reference to civil or canon law.

621 'My lord', he said, 'this is what God says–God who is truth, and you who sit in his place must so act in all things–God says: Ask righteously, and you shall receive; seek justly and you shall find; if you will knock at the true door, it shall be opened to you. We are weary and have come from far distant lands; we ask honestly for what we require. We ought to find here what we need. You will open the door to us; we knock rightly at it. You are in God's place; we shall find God in you'. When he had finished speaking, the Pope replied to him,

632 '*Frater*, you shall receive here what you have asked for; you have sought it rightly and you shall find it; we will open the door to you now, for you have knocked at it'. Then the pallium was brought forward. The Pope presented it to them, and they returned home with it. Thus Thomas obtained it without gifts and without sin; he did not give a penny for it, nor silver or gold. His successors in the see should follow his example.

God's Power Over All Men

641 How very mighty is God, how strong and how good, that he should have altered a human heart so suddenly. There is no king under heaven who has such power that he can change the heart or mind of any man under the sun against his will. But God changed him in a moment, when it was his pleasure and his will to do so, and made him suddenly hate what he was accustomed to love most dearly. From being bad, God made him good, and welcomed him among good men. Thomas repented deeply and grieved over the wrongs he had done. Such penitence smells sweet before God. No one, clerk or lay, should be surprised at this, nor stupidly imagine that God is unjust if sometimes he pulls men out of sin and sets them on their feet, and at others lets them stumble and die in it. He does not love wicked men, but holds good men dear. And God does not hate men themselves; he hates their folly, and he knows their whole hearts and all the course of their lives. He knows that this man will die in wickedness, that this other will die well, and he helps him immediately, the moment he repents and leaves his evil deeds. God knows very well all those who will be saved, and they, only, are destined to life. He knows too those who will be damned; it is not his purpose to summon them from their iniquity; they are destined to death, for they will end badly. Those who are to be damned, are destined to death; there is no appeal whatever from their damnation. And if God were to save them, he would be defrauding the devil. They will end in sin, they cannot make harbour. They will fall into the stinking whirlpool from which no one ever rises again.

671 God does not compel anyone to do right or to do wrong; he has given to every man free and equal strength so that each may use it as he wishes, for evil or for good. God loves and saves the man whom he finds to be loyal; he hates and damns the one whom he sees to be too carnal. When the eagle makes his young ones leave the nest, he makes them open their eyes towards the sun, and the one which cannot look at or endure its rays, he turns out of the nest and casts down. God will not nurture the man who refuses to love him. He has given intelligence, strength and power to all; he allows each one to act according to his own will. When a man neglects God in order to do wrong and expends his strength and intelligence in sin, would you then decide that God ought to have him? Look, there is the sentinel, high up on the mountain peak—he sees the thieves who have hidden themselves in the valley so as to catch the travellers who go along the road. And the travellers can see them too, they know that they will capture them, they knowingly get themselves caught by them. And we, we who thus insist on damning ourselves consciously, do you imagine God is going to save us by force? There he is up in heaven, watching what we do; he will come to judgment, to try good men and bad and he will let the devils lead away all those who serve them.

696 And then, if God were to save a single one of those who are to be damned, he would do wrong to the rest who are to perish for evermore. If he saves one, he ought by rights to save all. But the good and the bad will receive their right judgment and will be rewarded according to their deserts. And if anyone asks me why a man who is to be damned should do good, since it cannot help him, I reply, indeed, that he is mistaken—the worst man in the world could save himself if he would leave wrongdoing and turn to God. God the merciful calls us all to his kingdom, Saracen and pagan, Christian and Jew. One man is clear sighted, another blind; one is satisfied with little, another seeks great fiefs. According to each man's weakness, his place is made ready. One man loves his wife more than himself; to enrich his children, he forgets God, the king; he breaks the law many a time, to obtain riches, and he robs many of their inheritance; he steals and breaks his word, perjures himself, practises usury, and lives a life contrary to all law. And so no one must hesitate to do good, for in so doing everyone can free himself from pain; even those who are to be hopeless in hell for ever will be much eased by the good they will have done. So each man must work to save himself.

721 And so I tell you, my lords, leave off wrongdoing! Think about putting right all that you have done wrong. Do not sleep in your sins; think about preparing yourselves so that when God comes for you, you will be able to go with him and to climb with your lamps burning into paradise. And if you do not fear God, then fear hell, which burns, from which no one who enters it can ever escape by any contrivance. Consider the good men there have been, the many sinners whom God has drawn to himself, and the holy martyr Thomas, who was killed so recently. You have heard well enough what kind of man he was before—a man who would bite, like the wolf which took the lamb, an evil-doer, proud, seeking glory and renown—now he became sincere and gentle, he despised ermine and miniver. And the more he loved God, the worse was his relationship with the king. For as soon as he was consecrated to this honour, he made himself a proclaimer of God's word, and gave his whole attention to his sovereign lord. I do not know whether it was because of this that the king began to hate him, but it was from this time onwards that he banished him from his love.

CHAPTER TWO

Troubles

741 I CAN TELL YOU all about the first quarrel. The baron sent Master Ernulf[1] across the sea to the king with a message telling him that he was giving him back his seal. The king was furiously angry.

'God's eyes!' he said, 'will he not keep it any longer? I have got letters and full permission for him to be Archbishop and Chancellor simultaneously.'[2]

'He will not', Master Ernulf answered. 'He returns it absolutely to you, because he is very greatly occupied with his own work.'

'He doesn't care about serving me!' said the king; 'that's very clear.'

751 The second clash occurred at Woodstock,[3] and provoked the king into a blaze of anger against Thomas. There is a custom in England by which the sheriffs' aid is collected by counties; it is assessed at two shillings on every hide.[4] The barons of the country used to pay it to the men who were appointed to look after the counties, so as to protect their lands and their men and so that no one should sue them at law or do them any damage. Now the king wanted this diverted to his income.

'My lord', said the Archbishop, 'you must not seize the aids. You cannot convert them into revenue, for we are under no obligation to pay them if we do not want to, but since the sheriffs are able to be so useful to us, it would be wrong for us not to help them.'

'God's eyes!' he said, 'they shall all be enrolled. And you, you are to do my will; whatever pleases us shall be done with what is yours.'

'By those eyes', Thomas answered, 'by which you swore, not one shall ever be paid to you from my land.'

The Case of Philip de Broi

771 Then another time there was a serious conflict in London,[5] about a canon who lived at Bedford; he was Philip de Broi, who was accused—wrongly—of having killed a knight. The king wanted to send him to that port from which there is no return. In my opinion it was very wrong to harass him so, for he had pleaded his case for a long time in the bishop's court, and all his opponents had released him from it; yet he had also purged himself of it legally—and now the judge began the case against him all over again. Simon FitzPeter was the judge in charge of the case; he would have liked, if he could, to have got him killed.[6] Philip lost his temper and insulted him grossly; the king said that in offending him, it was just the same as if he had insulted the king himself. Those who killed God offended more seriously than did those who subsequently killed St. Peter or St. Vincent—but King Henry said what he wanted to say, and swore that he would have the judging of this clerk. Archbishop Thomas summoned him to his court and said that he would see to it that he was corrected, in his court. Whether the king liked it or not, he had to send bishops and barons there, to proceed against the clerk. He ordered them to give him full justice, if they feared for their eyes. They began by proceeding against him for the death of the knight. The clerk, while refusing to recognise that the case had been re-opened, said that he denied the murder entirely, as he had not done it, and added that he had already been released from this charge and had concluded the matter by purgation. He did not wish to open the case, either by a defence or by a withdrawal. Then they made him defend himself on the question of the insult. The clerk was a gentleman, and did not try to deny anything; he said he was perfectly willing to atone for his misconduct and would very gladly make full amends to the knight.

'Since he does not deny it', they said, 'we must pronounce judgment.'

806 They sentenced him to be deprived of his benefice for two years; the king was to have the income during this period, and would give it to churches, to the poor, to the upkeep of bridges and in other alms as it should please him. To what a mighty pursebearer Philip could now lay claim! Besides this, they said that he must strip himself in front of the knight, if the latter would allow it, and, with his friends as witnesses, must bring weapons, and on them must swear to him according to the law of the land; that was the kind of atonement that he would accept from him for that kind of offence.[7] When they reported the sentence to the king, he said they had acted very wrongly towards him, in that they had been lenient because the man was a clerk. He wanted them to have condemned him to death. They had given, they answered, an entirely just decision.

'God's eyes!' he said, 'I'll have that on oath. You shall swear to me that the decision you have given me is a loyal one.'

'My lord', said the bishops, 'you see us here ready to do so. But the sentence is too severe upon Philip.'

They offered the oath; the king broke into a storm of rage.

The Council of Westminster

826 Then[8] he summoned all the prelates to appear before him once more and wanted them to promise that they would keep and maintain the customs of the realm, which it was his duty to administer, and which his ancestor had established in his kingdom. 'Save their order', they said, they were willing to obey him in this.[9] The king insisted that they do it 'save their order' or not, and said that there was not to be a whisper of that expression. They declared unanimously that without the saving of their order, they would not do it, not for any reason. At this the king became angry with them, and he said he would not let them slip out of it by any means, for in his forefather's[10] time bishops and archbishops who had since become saints used to keep the customs. The Archbishop replied, 'I will not abandon the order'. None of the bishops would omit the phrase.

The holy man addressed all the bishops:

842 'You see', he said, 'how hard King Henry presses us. He wants to set up evil customs in holy church. It will be her disgrace if I establish them, but I am not strong enough to stand alone against the whole country. I would like to hear what each of you feels about this.' They all of them told him to stand firm, they would support him in everything; and they took an oath to do so. Roger of Pont l'Evêque also promised to stand by him; he would not fail him in any way.

851 Then the bishop of Lisieux[11] went to Salisbury. There had been some bitterness between him and the king, but now his behaviour towards the king made them friends. He gave the king such advice as would deceive his brother; he was the very fount and substance of the Archbishop's defeat.

'My lord', he said to the king, 'if you want to defeat him, get a party of the bishops onto your side. As long as they all stand by him, you will never get the better of him'. Hilary of Chichester was then sent for, and the king managed to retain his friendship; then he added Roger of Pont l'Evêque to his party, and got the bishop of Lincoln[12] to agree with his policy. He was at Colchester;[13] there they agreed that they would keep his customs, and he promised them that no word should in future ever be spoken against their order.

866 Then the bishop of Chichester went to Teynham,[14] to see the Archbishop. He hoped to get Thomas to eat out of the same dish that he was eating out of, and told him that he ought to be on good terms with his earthly lord; if he confirmed the customs, he could be his friend.

'You will never persuade me to it', replied the good priest. 'The king has persuaded Archbishop Roger and you to keep his laws, and so you want to add me as well, but you will never get me to join you.'

'My lord', he said, 'why not? For God's sake, now, explain to me why you would not do it and what you really think.'

'The king has promised you that he will make no demands on you that may be against your order. If he wants to, he will keep his word; if not, nobody is going to oppose him. But you, you will be compelled to keep what you have promised, for you are his men, and he will make you keep it.'

881 Then Robert of Melun[15] (so people called him), who then held the dignity of Hereford, went to the Archbishop at Harrow, taking with him John, Count of Vendôme;[16] he was a man whom Archbishop Thomas much respected. There was an abbot there too, who had come from across the sea: I have heard him called Philippe of l'Aumône.[17] He was to reconcile the Archbishop and the king; the Pope, he said, had sent him to do so, and he had brought a letter from him about this. He told the Archbishop and swore truly to him that he was Pope Alexander's messenger, to tell him to come to terms with the king, that he should do what the king required. He had given him good advice, considering the danger to his order, and he took full responsibility if he had in any way acted mistakenly. He had brought with him the cardinals' letters, and swore that the king had assured them that he sought nothing but that he should do him honour; and that he should, in the presence of his assembled barons, grant to him—by word of mouth only—what was asked of him. He would not be asked to keep, against his will, any customs contrary to his order. He did not want to be defeated over this, but let him grant him his will, and all anger on both sides would be forgiven. The king would make him absolute lord of the whole kingdom. And the king had loved him in times past better than any man, and he had served the king most loyally—so the abbot bewitched him with words, since he saw that he was a man of great authority, and persuaded him to go with him to Woodstock.

911 There they made him make his promise to the king, and concede that he would keep his customs in good faith, loyally; for he did not expect to hear them mentioned again. The king answered him: 'If you wish to consent, you must demonstrate the fact in the presence of all my barons. They have all heard how you have opposed me. If you intend to stand by the agreement you have made, summon all the clergy, and I will summon my barons; there shall be no delay. There, in the presence of all of them, declare what you have granted to me.'

The Meeting at Clarendon

921 The barons all assembled at Clarendon,[18] and the bishops were there in great numbers. The king wanted the Archbishop to declare in the hearing of all these witnesses what he had conceded to him. But the Archbishop regretted that he had gone so far. He was deeply sorry that he had authorised the keeping of a custom which was contrary to reason, and preferred to come into conflict with the king rather than throw holy church into confusion. Against God, he feared neither threats nor imprisonment. Unable to vanquish him, the king could only rage. He threatened to cut God's ordained priests to pieces; if he could, he would overthrow holy church. The Archbishop refused to humble himself in any way, whatever the king might threaten him with.

936 I do not know what the king and his party concocted, but two bishops now went direct to the Archbishop: Salisbury,[19] whom the king detested, and Norwich,[20] whom he had long disliked. They spoke to Archbishop Thomas:

'My lord', they said, 'for God's sake, have mercy on yourself, on all holy church, on the clergy, on us. The king is so furiously angry with you that if you do not make peace with him today, we shall both of us certainly lose our heads.'

946 This had no effect on the Archbishop; his purpose remained unchanged. Then two earls of that country went to see him: the Earl of Leicester,[21] a man of great good sense, and the Earl of Cornwall,[22] a friend of the king. They told him to have mercy both on himself and on his own men; to take care of holy church and of her clerks, because if he refused to do that day what the king wanted, then they would be forced to wreak such havoc with their own hands that they and the king would be dishonoured by it, as men without law. Even this considerable threat did not affect his courage.

956 Then two brethren went to him, men from across the sea: Sir Richard of Hastings, Master of the Temple, and Hostes as well, both well-known men.[23] They came before him in tears.

'My lord', they said, 'for the sake of God who never lied, why will you not take pity on holy church? Do what King Henry wants in this matter; confirm his customs; then you will be friends. Otherwise holy church and all clerks will be in real danger.' They were perfectly sure, quite certain, that if he granted what the king was asking for, the king would act on it entirely as he would wish; he would never hear a word spoken against his order; they pledged themselves and their loyalty to this. Might they, they said, be dead and damned if the king was contriving any trap or trickery towards him. Let him simply, in the presence of all his barons, fulfil his promise to him that he had denied; might this now be conceded! He wanted to avoid a defeat; it would disgrace him.

976 The Archbishop saw how hard they pressed him, he saw how very prone to sin were the king and his men, saw holy church in disaster, and himself and the clergy as well, and he supposed that he would regain the king's friendship. The men who had advised him were, he knew, very well thought of.

'My lords', he said then, 'I trust your opinion. Since you recommend it, I grant what he requires.'

Then they stood up, and he made his promise to the king in the hearing of all his barons. He said that he would maintain both customs and law in good faith and loyally.

986 'My lords', then said the king, 'you have all heard clearly that the Archbishop has promised me (and I thank him for it) that he will keep the laws of King Henry's time. Now I require that he make all the bishops here assembled confirm this as well.'

'My lord', the Archbishop said, 'I do indeed order them to do so'. Then they all arose and were granting this, when the bishop of Salisbury stood up and asked the Archbishop if he would do as much.

'Yes', said the Archbishop.

'Then so do I grant it', he said.

'You have always opposed me!' the king said to him. Then the king said, 'My lords, since they have agreed to keep the laws of our kingdom, it is now for you to take careful thought, so that in future no disagreement about the laws shall arise between us. Go out now and make a record for me of King Henry's laws; then write them down. When they are in writing, show them to us.'

1004 The king put all his wisest men to this task; they drew up the documents and brought them to the king. The text was then read out, in the whole crowd's hearing.

'My lords', said the king, 'I want there to be no new dissension. Let the Archbishop append his seal to this.'

'No!' said the Archbishop, 'by my duty to the God of glory, not while the soul still beats in my body!'

For those who had advised him to take this course, and the king's associates, had assured him that if he would confirm, verbally, this matter before the king, and would grant it to him in the hearing of all his barons, it would never at any time be recorded or written down; the king would do all that he wished about it, and all anger between the two of them would be forgiven. Now they went back on their word to him. He would do no more. Indeed, he had done too much already; he regretted that he had gone so far.

1021 And so the king's men thought of something else: they had a chirograph drawn up, and cut in two, and gave one half of it to the Archbishop: he accepted it, as a means of defending the clergy.[24] 'My lords', he said, 'this will enable us to see their wickedness. Now let us have a good look at the trap that we must beware of; they thought they could make holy church tumble into it.' Then the baron went away, and all he could do was to be angry that he had agreed to this deception, and had not been able to obtain the king's friendship.

1031 And because he had done wrong, he suspended himself from his functions and did not sing mass until he had sent to the Pope. He understood why he had behaved as he did, and released him from the suspension[25]—he had done it to free the king and the clergy, the one from evil and death, the other from sin.

But now the bishop of Evreux, called Rotrou,[26] as I have heard, went to Portchester[27] to reconcile the two men. The king said that he might go on talking about it for ever, if he could not manage to get the Pope to consent to put his seal to these laws. Through Bishop Rotrou, by whom he was much advised, the good priest wrote to the Pope and begged him to confirm the king's laws and to seal them. But he refused; he was well aware that Thomas had been forced to make this request.

Henry's Embassy to the Pope

1046 King Henry, seeing that he was thus totally rebuffed, was bitterly angry with the Archbishop, and began to plan how he should be made to yield; he now reinforced his plans with evil stratagems. He would gladly have taken vengeance, if only he could. Then both his barons and his intimates recommended to him that he should get the Pope to grant legatine powers to the Archbishop of York; then he would be able to subdue the Archbishop altogether; willy nilly, he would come to heel. He therefore sent two of his clerks to the Pope: John of Oxford[28] took much trouble over the affair, and Sir Geoffrey Ridel[29] prepared himself to deliver the message which was entrusted to them. They went to the Pope; he refused them. The church, he said, of Holy Trinity had been, and was, and ought to be of great authority; that of York had never had control of it, nor should it ever have, through him, while he lived. These two prelates had never behaved like friends. One of the messengers, however, was exceedingly cunning—kneeling before the Pope, he swore to him on sacred relics that if the king was not made happy by being granted this legation, as soon as he knew that they had returned to the country, he would make the Archbishop shorter by a head. But the Pope was a very intelligent man, who knew that is necessary to do wrong in order to prevent worse, and he said that he would grant the king legatine powers;[30] but none the less this should not enable him to harm anyone, nor to establish the Archbishop of York as legate. He would immediately write another letter and send it to a confidant of his in that land; if King Henry attempted to harass anyone by means of these legatine powers, he would see that he was forbidden to do so. The legation would never be any use to him. The king's messengers were intelligent men; when they saw how little they had obtained, they spoke as follows to Pope Alexander:

1084 'My lord, the king has been a good friend to you—you certainly ought to do what he asks you. For he is not asking this in order to depose anyone, but simply to check the Archbishop and if possible to make him come round to what the king wishes. He wants to be able to demonstrate to him in front of all his clergy that he very easily could harm him, if he wanted to.'

'You will get no other kind of legation', he answered.

He had his letter written and gave it to them. They returned to England, and showed the letter to the king. He, seeing that he could not get his own way, thought very poorly of it indeed, but none the less he frequently made a great display of it, making sure that the earls, barons and bishops should all see it, and would say to them, 'Look, I have got the legatine powers. Now I can make things difficult for the Archbishop!' But that was all the damage he could do him.

It annoyed the king extremely, not to be able to do the Archbishop any harm, and he sent the letter back to

Pope Alexander, and waged outright war on the clergy and holy church; he attacked the clergy in every way he could and showed a deadly animosity towards the Archbishop.

Criminous Clerks

1106 Another serious contention arose between him and the king, about such reckless clerks as were, by ill destiny, robbers, murderers and secret traitors. The king wanted to have the law of the land on them, but the Archbishop had obstructed that law. A law exists throughout the world, rightly established in Christendom and even in pagan lands, that a man caught stealing, or in any other such crime, should receive full and complete justice; no one must be spared, not for a father or a brother's sake. For this reason the king, and his barons as well, wished that when any ordained man was taken in wrongdoing—such as theft, murder or treason—he should first lose his orders for the offence and then be handed over to death and to mutilation. Several priests and deacons—thieves and murderers—had been arrested and put into the king's prisons. They were very often taken about the country in carts, and brought before councils where they were sentenced to mutilation, hanging or death. Thomas the Archbishop fought for them; he urgently demanded his lord's men. Suppose they had done wrong, he did not abandon them for that but maintained firmly that if anyone accused them, he ought to have them in the Lord God's court. The king refused to grant any point of this; he would not let them go by any means. What he wanted was that they should first be unfrocked; then he ordered that they should be handed over to the judge to be hanged or burned or dismembered alive. In his ancestor's time clerks taken in such foul crimes were dismembered; therefore he now insisted on having his ancestor's customs and usages maintained absolutely, without infringement; the Archbishop was not to hear one more case—if he did, he would regret it. The Archbishop replied that it should never be so; he would never hand clerks over to lay justice, but would always defend them according to God and to right, and would do justice to them properly according to canon law. He would not allow holy church to be brought down on his account.

1146 'Clerks', he said, 'are not bound to obey your laws, nor ought they to suffer twice for one offence–losing their orders, and then perishing physically. That is why I intend to support them wholeheartedly, as is reasonable. You can never make me yield over this. Certainly I concede to you that all clerks found committing such crimes should be unfrocked, but after that they should be pronounced safe as to their limbs. If they are taken again after that, then let them be blinded, skinned, or hanged, as you will. The true model of justice is not to be found in men who act of their own authority in all that they do, nor in those who are and always have been in the world, but rather in men to whom God has given his holy spirit. Otherwise one would be odds with God. When King David,[31] in whom the Holy Spirit dwelt, established his son Solomon as king, many of the people opposed him, and they chose his son Adonijah to be king. Abiathar wanted to consecrate him, scorning God; and because he had thus acted against God and against reason, he was led before King Solomon for judgment. But the king would not order him to be dismembered; instead he told him to go and dwell in his own house. He did, however, suspend him completely from his post. No one should suffer twice for one offence. When a clerk is unfrocked, no one can impose any further disgrace on him. It is my duty to defend holy church and the clergy, and defend them I will, for the sake of God to whom I owe service. Not for life or for death will you see me budge.'

1176 When King Henry realised that he could not make him give way and that he would not allow guilty clerks to be dismembered, he blazed at him in a fury, and promised him faithfully that he would bring him down, he would put him back where he had taken him from.

This struggle between the two men lasted a long time. King Henry could not make the Archbishop submit; he continued to defend those unhappy, reckless clerks, and he fought alone, for he had few friends. Almost all the bishops had gone over to the king. They had left him all alone in the heat of the battle, they had given the horn into the hand of the sinner,[32] and were too frightened to draw the sword of God. They dreaded an earthly lord more than they did Jesus, the mighty creator.

Garnier Addresses the Bishops

1191 You weak and foolish men! Tell me, what is it you are afraid of? That the king will take your powers from you? Indeed, he will not, if you have the courage to hold on to them. You are not real bishops, you are only called so. You do not do your duty in any respect. You ought to lead other men and keep them on the right path, but you make them all stumble and fall—you even make the king of the country go wrong. You ought not always advise him to follow his own wishes; no, you should often rebuke and reprimand him. God has entrusted his flock to you for protection, and if the king is your sheep, then you must lead him. The shepherd must always turn away the stranger and carry the sick sheep on his shoulder; he must not leave it for the robber to kill. You are hirelings; there are not many true shepherds. And the king can see this, he will think all the worse of you. God, who placed him in the kingdom, will require him at your hands; it is your duty to keep him well. He will not always think as he does now, and then he will hate those who gave him this advice. The king's duty is to govern the people of this world, and he wants to have such laws as will best please him. Laymen want their laws and customs established as their fathers had them before them. But God is of heaven, and so are his laws. Let me ask both king and clergy this: which laws ought Christians to keep better, those set up by Saracens and Slavs and people in the world, or those that holy men have had written down?

1221 Take fresh thought, king, don't rely on bad counsel. They are false, these prelates whom you have entrapped, more pliant than reeds in a storm of wind.

They deceive their own lord—will they be true to you? Do not trust the night; give yourself to the sun. Allow holy church to possess her laws and her rights—she is the bride of God, and God is lord of kings. He will be angry if you diminish her in any way. He will suffer you for a year, or two or three, 30, 20 or 10—or for a week, a day, a month. If Nero were alive now, he would soon find Simon,[33] who beguiled everyone with his words and his bribes. Rome was the house of God; now it is a den of thieves. Moses stands all alone in Pharaoh's kingdom, he can find no trace of his brother Aaron.[34]

The Status of Clerks

1236 Clerks are God's servants, chosen by him, called to be his saints—their name says as much. Whatever they may be, they are servants in God's household and it is not for you to touch them, not even the least little clerkling. He is, if you look at it rightly, given to God. King, you may be anointed and wear a golden crown, but it is with righteousness that you must shine, not pride. You must be the head and the guardian of your people. You will not take it away with you, you were not born wearing it. The glory of this world does not last long. A clerk bears his sign on his head all the time; it does not trouble his body but it weighs upon his soul. From near or far, he is shaved like a lunatic. He must never behave proudly towards anyone, or violently, but must be humble to all men and bring peace wherever he goes. A clerk is God's throne; God must be seated in him. He must always be learning, there is so much he has to know. In every situation he must show discretion and wisdom. Yet God has not made him proof against his own sins; he is human, and they can deceive him.

Clerks must protect laymen and their souls. No one may condemn his superior, clerk or lay, and that is why one superior is put in authority over another. A man who has done wrong must be handed over to his superior; he must be dealt with according to the same law that he lives by. Guilty clerks shall be delivered to the bishops.

And how, by what method, are they to be dis-ordained? How are the words of that sacrament to be removed? Who can unconsecrate what God has consecrated? To my mind this is not law, but a capricious ruling. An unfrocked man who can get to Rome and obtain the Pope's forgiveness and permission simply to sing mass does not delay a moment before he celebrates mass—the Pope does not have him re-ordained. No one can deconsecrate what God has consecrated, nor de-Christianise any Christian man (although of course he can be cut off from holy church).

1274 I by no means recommend that such a man, once arrested, should be allowed to go free and to continue his former kind of life. A wicked man does not fear the loss of his orders—little does he care about orders, a man who murders people, steals other men's goods, takes them by force. He fears neither dishonour nor death, gallows nor torture. Set such a man free once he is taken, and he will never improve. A wicked man is like the wild boar you have heard tell of in Avianus,[35] the one who used to spoil the rich man's wheat. He was caught in it twice and they let him go, although they cut off his ears first. When he was captured, the owner told him never to come back there again; if ever he did, he assured him, he would pay for it. Then they marked the boar and let him go. But he would not be warned—he was caught a third time in the wheat. This time they killed him, and gave him to the cook. The cook ate the boar's heart, and when he was asked for it, he made the lord believe that the boar had been born without a heart, for if he had had one, he would have reflected. A wicked man is always wicked, and will never learn wisdom. So I feel it reasonable to say and indeed to assert that if a clerk be condemned to lose his calling, his superior should then have him thrown into his prison and never let out again—he can amend his misdeeds there, if he likes.

1301 Adam, after God had created him and set him in paradise, was not killed for what he had done wrong but was put into the prison of this painful world; he lived all his life out in pain and sorrow, to atone for the wrong he had done. Both Adam and the clergy have no other head than God, so that this seems to me to be a fair comparison. And if a clerk is ever caught committing such crimes, then let his superior throw him into his prison—the king may trust my reasoning. It is right for earthly law to spare no one, in its efforts to control and punish criminals, but God's pity turns no one away. He wants the sinner to live, that he may cleanse himself, leave his wickedness and turn to God. This is clearly shown in Adam, who was the first man who ever did wrong: God clothed him in skins and made both him and us subject to death; in Adam's labours he cursed our clay, which brings forth sins for us and so little good—but he did not curse the soul, that it should not return to heaven. God exiled Cain, who killed his brother, and with him separated excommunicates from good men; he cursed the earth which swallowed the blood from the sinner's hand, but he spared the soul; he excommunicated those who spill their neighbour's blood. Nebuchadnezzar had a great image of himself made out of silver and gold and compelled everyone in his kingdom to adore it; those who would not, he had killed or tortured—then God made him into an ox that ate grass. But when the seven years were up, God made him human again. We often see that the very worst sinner becomes simple and good and completely repentant, an example of goodness to great and small. God restores to him the glory of heaven, which till then he was losing. Seven devils dwelt within Mary; at God's feet she washed her sins away with her tears, she wiped and cleaned them away with her hair. At whatever time the penitent may be judged, he is saved by the love of God and of his neighbour. St. Peter the apostle, who holds the power both in heaven and in earth, denied God three times and said he did not know him. He thrust out his sin and wept bitterly and God forgave him. Anyone who sincerely begs for forgiveness, will receive it. It has never been heard of, nor found in writing, that a sinner who begged for mercy failed to obtain it. (Although if he despairs or drowns himself or kills himself, he cannot be forgiven, as he has sinned in the spirit.) God has chosen mercy above all else.

1351 And since God loves merciful justice so dearly and prefers forgiveness to sacrifice, the good Archbishop undertook this battle on behalf of the clergy and his mother church. He saw clearly that no lay hand ought to take it up.

Thomas Tries to Leave England

1356 The Archbishop realised that he would not be able to win back the king's affection, for Henry hated Thomas to the point of killing him, and was not a man to allow his hatred, once entered on, ever to be altered; and so Thomas prepared for a journey, and put to sea, sailing from Romney.[36] When they had sailed well out from land, the sailors who were there consulted together, and they spoke to Adam of Charing,[37] saying that they were out of their minds, to be taking the king's enemy out of the country, that they and their kinsfolk would lose all they had. They went all together to the Archbishop and told him that they could not sail against the wind; no one could cross the sea against that wind.

1369 'If the weather drives us back', he said, 'make harbour wherever God brings you'. The Archbishop has often spoken of this afterwards, in these terms; as far as he knew, they had put back because of the wind. God had not yet prepared him to make the crossing, nor had he yet stood in the narrow lists nor in the great battle, from which God delivered him. But when the king heard that he had nearly crossed, he was very upset and extremely anxious. He feared Thomas, on account of his intelligence, and was afraid he would go to the Pope, and that the whole kingdom would be put under an interdict. But his failure to get out of the country made no difference; the king still could not make him give way over any point.

CHAPTER THREE

Northampton

1383 KING HENRY set up his council at Northampton,[1] and summoned to it prelates and barons, all the men who owed him service in chief. Earls and barons, bishops and abbots went to this council all together.

1388 Archbishop Thomas did not refuse to attend along with the rest of the baronage, but the baron went there in great humility.[2] The king's men, who were well aware of all that was planned, had had their horses stabled where Thomas was to have stayed, and he told the king that he would not plead in his court until he had had all his lodgings cleared for him—then both horses and squires were ejected. The baron was summoned for a particular day, to be ready to answer there in person.

1398 The king had established a system in the kingdom, which is proving very harmful to the barons of the land, whereby a man can lose his court through a false oath.[3] If anyone brought a case in his lord's court concerning land, he was to go there with his people on the first day; if anyone delayed his case, he was to go to the judge and make his complaint; then come back again, bringing two witnesses with him. In his lord's court, he and the two others were to swear that the court had withheld from him his full rights. By means of such an oath, honest or dishonest, the man would now proceed to the court of his next lord, and so on until he would come to the court of his sovereign lord.

1411 John the Marshal[4] was bringing such a case. He had laid claim to a holding[5] in Saint Thomas's court, and as he had no right to it and was making no progress he took his court from him by means of an oath of this kind. He appealed about it to the king, who was seeking to harm him. The king summoned Saint Thomas there to plead, to be ready on the given day, and to defend himself upon a charge of having refused his full rights to John. He was ill that day, and could not sit a horse; he sent two of his men to present his excuses.[6] The king refused to accept his excuses, and that is why he made the Archbishop go to Northampton. The baron went there—he had no intention of doing otherwise—and stayed with the monks of St. Andrew. Next day he had a grievous burden to bear, for he went to the king to ask permission to go, as he told him, across the sea to the Pope. This was because Roger of York was having his cross carried everywhere in his parish, which the baron would not endure; they had appealed over the matter, and it was therefore necessary for him to go. And so on that next day he went to King Henry and at once asked his permission to go to the Pope. The king said he was not to go but must immediately answer for this delay. He said that he had been ill and had excused himself. But no illness or excuses were any use to him: the king said he meant to get his decision on the matter. They proceeded to judgment, with no intention of considering justice, and like undiscerning fools they condemned the Archbishop to pay £300 for pardon. The baron wanted to challenge their sentence, but they all most earnestly begged him to put aside his anger, accept their sentence, and do what the king wanted; thus he would be able to achieve a reconciliation with him. So they got him to agree to this sentence, and find sureties to the king for the £300. He found them at once—there was nothing else he could do. And after he had done so, they opened proceedings against him and began accusing him over the case of this man John. The baron replied that he did not wish to answer there, because this man had been in his court and had not been able to show that any wrong was done him; and when he wanted to leave it, he refused to make his oath on any other book than a book of tropes[7] which he had had brought in. It is not the custom in this country to swear on a book of tropes, but to kneel before the four gospels; he hoped, however, to deceive God by this kind of oath. But within that year the worms ate his flesh, and the bodies of his two sons,[8] whom he loved.

1461 The king would extend no indulgence to him at all, but required him, he said, to let him hear the accounts of all that he had had in charge when he was his Chancellor. The Archbishop answered that he did not wish to plead about this, as no day had been fixed for him to produce his accounts. The king sent a message to him saying that he was to be ready the next day to answer and to render his accounts in full. The Archbishop, who was no coward, replied that it was not a reasonable day on which to hold a fair deliberation. The king swore, God's eyes! he should appear next day. Thomas saw that he would never win King Henry's love, and fell at his feet and begged his mercy. He acknowledged that the king had made him and raised him: let him not now destroy what he had created.

1475 'God's eyes!' he said, 'now you have shamed me!' He went away into the other room, sweating and grey-faced with rage. He summoned all the other bishops to him, and the Archbishop remained alone, like some lost wanderer.

1480 'By God's eyes', he said, 'tell me what you recommend. Archbishop Thomas has been my servant, he has received all my rents over several years, and now, because he is Archbishop, he refuses to give me accounts of them or of anything else. Let me hear your opinions.' Not one of them said anything; he found each one silent. Seeing them all dumb, he was very angry.

1487 'For God's eyes', he said, 'do you refuse me your advice?' Then he turned to the bishop of Winchester. 'My lord and father', he said, 'you, what have you to say to me about this? You are the oldest; it is your duty to counsel me.'

1491 'Since you have asked me, my lord', said the bishop, 'I will tell you exactly what I think. He has not been subject to your laws since the day he was consecrated.

He will not render an account to you, even though he was your deputy. You must look to it more sharply; you will not destroy him by this means.'

1496 Then the king was furiously angry, because they did not pronounce in favour of his wishes. He went back into the room in a foul humour. The Archbishop rose to meet him, and went to his feet like a servant boy. All the other bishops fell at his feet; they prayed for the Archbishop, but he was in no way placated—he looked at them, ranked all round him, and exclaimed, 'God's eyes! Why do you shame me so? Never was anyone so dishonoured by his own men!'

1506 The Archbishop could see that he would get no further respite. As the evening drew on, he went to his lodgings. The pain in his side attacked him, and lasted all day and night. He was subject to it, and it often distressed him; it came back now because of the anxiety he was suffering.[9]

1511 Next day, however, the king sent for him in the morning, and swore by God's eyes he would have his accounts. He said he could not go, he was sweating with pain; if it pleased God, he said, his pain would pass, and he would go to court as soon as he could. The king swore by the eyes that he would be forced to attend, and whether he wanted to or not, must produce his accounts. The iller he was, the more harshly he pressed him. Archbishop Thomas sent back to him: for the love of God who made all the world, to bear with him. King Henry, realising that he could not make him come, thought that he was pretending to be ill, so as to deceive him. He sent two earls to see how ill he was: the Earl of Leicester, a man well known to be intelligent; and the Earl of Cornwall, to report the truth to him. They arrived there, and saw that he was ill. They gave him the king's message: that he was to go to court. He pointed out to them that his illness had caused him serious distress all night and had not yet left him, although he had sweated a little, and he begged them for God's sake to let him lie; if the king would bear with him till next day, he would go to court then, and listen to his will; he would not fail to go, not if it killed him. If necessary he would have himself carried there on a stretcher. They allowed him this much respite, in the king's name, and told him that the king would certainly insist next day on hearing his accounts; nothing would dissuade him from this. He would be there, he said. Then they left him, and made their report to the king.

1541 That same day he received another message, and was told for certain by two great barons that if he went to court he ought to be prepared—he would be put in prison, and never see his own feet again, or he would be killed; it was unavoidable. Hearing this, his flesh crawled. He went and told a holy man what had been said, and he advised him that next morning, when he served God, he should sing the mass of St. Stephen, the first martyr; then his enemies would not be able to hurt him. The baron rose next day at dawn (for the pain of his illness had passed off) and sang that mass very devoutly; he set forth his case before God his lord, and prayed he would protect him from evil fortune. (And yet later on, the bishop of London, speaking on behalf of the king, turned this mass which he then sang into an accusation against him before the Pope, saying that he sang it for sorcery, and in contempt of the king. But he strayed from the truth.) However, when he had sung mass, he did not unrobe, but sat down there, dressed as he was.[10] He sent his men to summon the bishops. When they came, he spoke eloquently to them as follows:

1565 'My lords', he said, 'for God's sake, advise me. The king's anger has built up against me to such a pitch that no one can say how serious a hurt he, and the best men in the empire, are planning to inflict on me. You are well aware of this, you can see to what end he is striving. No one but the Lord God can give me any remedy. And so I am very anxious and in real fear, for I know the king's secret intention—some of his closest confidants have told me of it in good faith. Therefore I mean to go to court dressed as I am now, carrying my cross in my hand, so as to ensure my safety.' One of them answered—one who was far from being distressed at this, who welcomed and encouraged the king's plans—

1578 'My lord, whatever do you mean to do? Surely you will not create such a scandal as to go to court with a drawn sword in your hand? If you do, the quarrel will never be ended. If you go to court like that, with your sword drawn, your hauberk on, spear in hand, anger and enmity will arise between you and the king; no one will ever be able to reconcile you; there will never be a day when holy church will not weep for it. You are already seriously at odds with the king; if you go to court like that, you will do him grave dishonour. You are looking for a fight, if you go armed. And your sword is blunt, but his is sharp—if he draws his sword on you, you will not be able to stand up to it. Lay down your cross, have yourself unrobed; have your cross carried in front of you. You must go very humbly to court, so that no one can possibly reproach or blame you. Then there will be more hope of being able to discuss peace with the king.'

The baron replied very humbly,

1597 'I have drawn no sword, I am not attacking him. I will not hand the cross to anyone, whoever may regret it. I seek peace; it distresses me that anyone should withhold it from me; and I would be deeply grieved if holy church were to weep for this. Neither do I wish any evil or dishonour to the king—there is no one in all the world who longs more eagerly for his honour, and I am very sad that he hates me. And if his sword is sharp, mine is unyielding. I must obey the sovereign lord. Now I request and command you that you give me such advice as may enable me to avoid disgrace before God and before the world.'

1608 'Do, my lord', said one of them, 'do humble yourself; surrender the archbishopric into the king's grace. It is the only way to peace, be sure of that.'

'You give me bad advice', he said, 'I will never do that.

Go on to the court now; I will get ready. God willing, I will abide by the truest counsel.' Then he at once took off his alb, keeping on, as I know for certain, his cope and surplice, and went, since he had been sent for, to the king's court. He armed himself with a stole, worn over his surplice, with a canon's cope on top, for he knew well enough how seriously he was at odds with the king. He mounted his horse, and commended himself to God. He deeply feared the king, and his savage anger, for he knew him very well, having worked for him so long, and he was well aware that the king hated him vehemently and that he would have but few friends at the forthcoming meeting.

1626 I find it very puzzling that the king should have been so bitter against him, unless it was because he had left his employment, withdrawn entirely from his confidence, and gone away from him; also that he dared to stand up to him, in anyway whatever. Thomas was not noble, his friends were not powerful; and the king, having raised him so high and shown him such affection as to take him into his complete confidence, never encountered anyone who angered him more. He felt that he was deeply slighted by the man he had made. A king's anger is no game for children. If he once begins to hate a man, for a trivial or a serious reason, he will never love him again all the days of his life. The king's wish is law, so some say, and all men obey their earthly lords. But God's vassal had left his earthly lord, and given himself utterly to God, his creator, whom he longed to serve in love and fealty. He knew that he would have to endure a grievous struggle; he feared imprisonment rather than loss of honour.

1646 Saint Thomas the good priest went to court, taking upon him the armour of God, for his safety's sake. He had the archiepiscopal cross carried on his right, and held the reins in his left hand. Christ Jesus, his master, he took as his advocate. He dismounted just outside the hall and went inside—someone held his horse —and found the hall full of people, young and old. Once in, he took the cross in his own hand. (The king was in his room, with his closest confidants.) Thomas went in, with very few companions; he took only a few of his own men with him, we are told, and went to the king amongst all his friends and associates—bishops, abbots, earls and barons. He entered the field alone, like a brave champion. The bishops stood up as he came in; they blamed and rebuked him for carrying the cross, for in so doing he dishonoured his lord the king—it would produce great enmity between them, let him hand it to someone else, they told him. Robert of Hereford went and asked him for it: he was a bishop, he said, he could very well entrust it to him. The bishop of London laid claim to it: he was his dean, he said, and ought rightly to carry it—he tried to force it out of his hands.

1671 'You always were a fool', he said, 'and you still are and always will be, attacking the king with a drawn sword. If he draws his sword on you, how are you going to defend yourself? You are doing him great dishonour, coming into his court in fire and flames, armed with your cross. But put it down, give it to someone else; don't infuriate our lord the king.'

1678 'Leave him alone, my lord bishop', said the bishop of Worcester,[11] 'let his cross be, you will not take charge of it. He is not too good to carry the cross which you see.'[12] They tried hard to get it from him, but he would not relinquish it to any of them and gripped it fast with both hands. Hardly any of the bishops supported him, except Roger of Worcester, who would not abandon him. Archbishop Thomas went forward, carrying the archiepiscopal cross in his own hands; he would not surrender it to anyone, for he apprehended great danger. He sat down on a bench and leaned upon God. He held the cross in his hand; he carried it in his heart.

1691 The king was sitting with his companions in the further room, holding discussions with his closest friends. The Archbishop did not go to him there, as the king was so enraged against him; they carried on all their business that day by means of intermediaries. Anger and unsound advice had misled the king, stirring him up so violently against the holy man. He had known the kind of man Thomas was, in times gone by, and did not realise that he had changed—but he was completely transformed, the Holy Spirit was in him.

1701 Now the king wanted to proceed against Thomas over the question of the clerks, but the barons got him to set that business aside, for if he were now to attempt any attack on the clergy he would find that all the bishops would rally against him, and then he would not be able to make the Archbishop give way.

1706 Thomas sat there on the bench, and the barons went to and fro between him and the king, two at a time, three at a time. He was told secretly by the king's closest confidants that his death was prepared, let him look out for himself; several swore to him that this was true. I do not know whether the king had arranged this, suggesting that he meant to have the Archbishop killed or bound, but people kept coming and telling him that it was so, all day. Possibly the king wanted to frighten him, thinking he would be better able to overcome him by threats.

1716 Then King Henry called the bishops to appear before him, and spoke strongly to them, insisting that they keep what they had promised him and observe the customs and the laws of the country—and the Archbishop was not to evade doing so. The bishops went to consult the Archbishop about it; they told him that they must keep the king's laws, for the Archbishop himself had made them accept them on their obedience, and confirm them *in veritatis verbo.* They did not want to be in any way disloyal to him. He himself, they said, must keep them, for he had accepted them, he had no business to draw back; he had given his word and could not break it. And the king now required to hear and know whether he intended to withdraw from his loyalty to him.

1731 Saint Thomas listened attentively to everything they said, then answered them very humbly. God, he said, was present in the man who loved truth; anyone who did not love loyalty, did not love God either. God hated all deceit and all wickedness. 'And those laws which you say the king insists on, have nothing to do with loyalty, but on the contrary with wickedness; they are against God, against reason, their purpose is to destroy the clergy. I will not keep them for any man alive. On holy obedience, I forbid you to keep them. A man who falls down is a fool if he does not get up again; it is better to get up quickly, not stay down too long. And since this court is determined to harass me—and you too, who in reason ought to stand by me—I now appeal, for I will not go against reason.'

1746 The Archbishop saw, and reflected.[13] He would have to appeal to the papal court and see if he could deliver himself by that means. He saw all the bishops standing about him—not one of them would utter a word, because of the king. He realised clearly that his life was sought, and he saw all the bishops standing round him—

'My lords', he said, 'I appeal, for my need is great. This court is persecuting me.'

'My lord', said the bishop of London, 'excuse me from this.' The bishop of London said,

1756 'Hold me excused from this, my lord.'

'No, I will not', he replied. 'But I command you all to do justice for it if I am touched; do not on any account spare anyone concerned.' The bishop of Winchester was very much distressed.

'My lord', he said, 'do now for God's sake listen to me: surrender the archbishopric into the king's mercy. It is your only hope of peace, I can see it clearly.' He said this in all sincerity, not out of any evil intention—he could see great danger arising, and deadly enmity.

1766 'No, I will not', he answered. 'Never, so long as I live, will I surrender divine office into a layman's hands; it would be against God and against loyalty.' The bishop of Chichester said,

'If I could have my way, you would be just plain Thomas, without this authority.'

When the majority realised Archbishop Thomas's danger, they were deeply sorry, and called out to Archbishop Roger, to the bishop of London, who hated him, and to Chichester, who had never been a friend of his, saying,

1776 'My lords, for the love of God, don't do it. If they kill the Archbishop, you will be blamed, for the whole country knows how you hate him. If you do not save him, we shall all be in trouble—the king and holy church and we ourselves will all be disgraced.' Then the bishops went and consulted together, to see if they could contrive to deliver him. They said they would go and talk to King Henry; if they were to appeal against Thomas to the Pope, they would thus be able to get him deposed from his see. They went to the king about it, and implored his mercy.

1787 'My lord', they said, 'for God's sake, do not do this. Put a stop to this matter that you have begun, for it will always redound to your discredit, and we shall be disgraced and suspended. My lord', they said to the king, 'let us deal with it. You know how he made us confirm your laws, and now he is trying to make us all break faith; we are going to accuse him on these grounds, unanimously, and so we shall be able to get him deposed from his see.'

'I agree', said King Henry, 'let it be so.'

1797 'Leave it to us', they said; 'we shall take great care over it; we shall bring down his pride, whether he likes it or not.' Some of them meant well, others ill. Then they went to see him. They were all very agitated.

'We appeal', they said, 'for we have too much to bear. You have now forbidden what we had previously granted to the king, what you yourself had commanded on our obedience. You are trying to make us be disloyal, and so we have appealed against you.'

1806 King Henry's councillors told him about all this,[14] and when he heard that he had made an appeal and gone utterly against his wishes—I cannot tell you what his thoughts and feelings were! But he did not hide them from his councillors.

Then they said to him,

'My lord, you must leave this matter alone. Trust our advice and he will lose the archbishopric; we'll bring him down. He wants to make us break our word to you, to deceive you, and we mean to challenge him about it before the Pope.'

'Do it at once then', he said; 'start thinking about it.'

Then they went and spoke to him, and he listened; they said:

1818 'My lord, as you are leading us so far astray, making both us and yourself disloyal to the king, we appeal. You have pressed us too hard.' By means of this appeal they succeeded in reassuring the king and for the time being they pacified his anger. He thought that as Thomas had denied what he had earlier acknowledged, he would, if this were proved against him in God's court, lose his crosier and his high office. I believe that the prelates of York and of London both advised him privately not to do him any harm when there were so many people about to see it, but to send for him the next day, when no one would be there; then he would be able to lock him away quietly without any disturbance. And so the king's anger was cooled and the wicked plot that had been prepared was brought to nothing; their evil contrivance resulted in great good. For whatever a man may purpose, his power is but feeble. God brings down powers and evil plans.

1836 Then the king sent his knights to him and demanded that he render full account to him of all that he had been in charge of when he was his Chancellor, of £30,000 sterling, in pence. But he answered the messengers very finely, saying:

1841 'My lords, I say—without acknowledging that any plea has been begun—that my lord has no right to ask for my accounts. I employed this very large sum that you mention in his business; and my lord has often heard it accounted for. Moreover, when I was raised to this dignity in London, I was declared—by his own orders, as you very well know—quit and free of all claims connected either with accounts or with any other matter. I do not therefore wish to re-open this plea, which has already been concluded.' When they reported these words to the king, he went red with rage, redder than a hot coal in a fire, and said:

'By God's eyes, he refuses to render his accounts? And he is my liege man! I will have judgement on him!'

1855 'Yes, my lord', they said, 'but on other grounds, where he has acted even more wrongly: since he is your liege man he ought to keep faith with you and always protect your honour and defend it—if he tries to take your court from you and denies its competence by appealing to another court, you can attack him on those grounds, for this is an attempt to do you grave dishonour. You can sentence him for this', the barons said to him.

1862 'Proceed to judgment, then', he said, 'without loss of time.' And so Nero's household went to judgment and like lunatics they sentenced their spiritual father, condemning him to be arrested and imprisoned by the king.[15] Archbishop Roger left this council meeting, and said to the Archbishop:

'Have pity on yourself and on us; we shall all be in great trouble if you do not do exactly what King Henry wants.'

'Be gone, Satan', Saint Thomas said to him.

1871 When the sentence was agreed upon, and had been pronounced and recorded before the king, the king sent to him two of his close confidants, Reginald, Earl of Cornwall, and the Earl of Leicester, a most intelligent man. They went straight to the Archbishop together, and stopped in front of him. The Earl of Leicester spoke first:

'My lord', he said, 'the king has sent to you by us to require you to hear the sentence that has been agreed concerning you.' The good priest looked at him proudly—

'I will listen to no sentence this day', said the good Archbishop, 'for I have appealed.'

'How can it be averted', asked the Earl, 'when you owe him fidelity, homage, and allegiance? You hold great estates and great fiefs of him in barony, and since this is so, you must accept the law and the sentence of his court.'

1888 'I hold from him', Saint Thomas answered, 'neither fief nor inheritance nor anything at all in barony; all the fiefs I hold are held in charity and in perpetual alms. All that his ancestors ever granted to holy church was given in perpetual alms; no word of barony was ever suggested. The king has confirmed it all by his charter, granting it as alms, in perpetuity. Therefore', he said to them, 'in God's name I forbid you, by that christianity which comes to you from us, to pass any sentence on me this day.'

1899 'In the face of such a prohibition', answered the Earl, 'I will have nothing more to do with it. I declare you free of any obligation.' And then Earl Robert went on, 'You pronounce it, Earl Reginald; I do not dare do it, when he forbids it so strongly.'

'Neither will I, so the Lord God save me', the Earl replied. 'The task was not given to me, I am not going to exceed my commission. You say it if you want to, for Reginald will not help you.'

'My lord', said Earl Robert, 'for St. Denis's sake, be patient, until King Henry has heard your answer.'

'What', asked Archbishop Thomas, 'am I a prisoner?'

'No, by St. Lazarus, you are not', the good Earl replied.

1910 'Then I shall go now', answered the friend of God. These two great vassals went back to the king, and the holy Archbishop left the place where he had been sitting; he went quickly out of the royal chamber, taking with him no companion but God the spiritual, and carrying the archiepiscopal cross in his right hand. And as he left the king's room, barons and justices, such as I ought not to mention by name, raised a hue and cry against him, shouting out 'The traitor's going, look at him, look at him!' He walked on, not uttering a word. Even Earl Hamelin[16] did not keep quiet: when he saw Archbishop Thomas leaving, he shouted at him noisily, yelling out 'Away you go like a criminal, you wicked traitor!' Hugh Wake[17] too, he all but wore himself out, shouting at him. Thomas left the room as fast as he could; then, crossing the hall, he stumbled over some firewood and nearly fell—at that, Ranulf de Broc[18] yelled at him, exclaiming 'There goes the traitor!' The holy man did not say a word, but went on his way. Loud shouts of 'Traitor!' came at him from every side of the hall—had the city tumbled down, the uproar could have been no greater. They even flung handfuls of straw after him. He would not enter into debate with them; he went on his way.[19]

1936 The Jews did just the same when God was condemned—they screamed filth at him, they beat and battered him, they spat in his face. God endured it of his own free will, for human sin; and so too did this man, to free the clergy from wretchedness.

1941 Bad men, who thought they were pleasing the king—and servant lads and sluts—raised this uproar against Saint Thomas, and threw lumps of straw at him, because Ranulf had suggested it. But the men who feared God, and who had once loved him, groaned to see him so treated, and wept secretly.

1946 Then someone told the king how they were in full cry after the Archbishop, that they would injure and kill him; the king's honour would suffer if he were not left alone. So then the king ordered and had it proclaimed that the Archbishop and his men were to be allowed to depart in safety.

1951 As soon as the baron had leapt onto his horse, he rode fast to the gate, and found it shut; this dismayed him, for he was afraid he would be caught and held prisoner. But God delivered him, miraculously—the Archbishop had his squire with him, a man called Trunchet,[20] and this man was a real help to him. He noticed the bunch of keys hanging some distance away on a branch, and he grabbed them quickly, not wanting any delay, and opened the gate, without calling for the porter. God did not intend to leave the Archbishop there. Out of as many keys as this man could hold in both hands, he immediately took the right one. The porter was busy beating some vagabond—the baron, beloved of God, went out through the gate.

1966 The Earl of Leicester heard the outcry and told the king how the Archbishop was being mobbed; it was shameful that so high placed a man should be attacked like this; he ought not to allow it; it would be a reproach to him. Then the king ordered them to leave him alone.

1971 When Thomas got back, he dismounted and went into the monastery church, asking if it was time to sing nones. It was later than that, however, so he sang nones and vespers, for he never forgot God's service, early or late. He delighted in serving him, and God has rewarded him. Then after that he came out of the church, called for his servants, and asked for food. All his clerks and his knights had fled—he could not have found half a dozen if he had needed them. Fear of the king had scattered them. Then Thomas ordered that the poor be brought in; they filled up the refectory tables with them. I imagine he had other things to think of than filling his stomach, but he ate a sufficient amount, at leisure, and appeared cheerful, to encourage his men.

1986 Night had fallen and it was quite dark while he was still at table. They carried his bed into the church, as everybody observed, and made it up behind the high altar, setting his lambskin cloak up over the pillow, and turning back the cover a little. When the monks came in to sing their compline, they were sure the baron was fast asleep, and sang softly so as not to distress him, telling one another by signs not to go near, he was tired out, they must not disturb him. He had stationed one of his own men there to guard the bed; when anyone went near it, he told them to go back again, and said they were to let his lord rest. Not a soul would have gone and looked—they expected to find him still there next day. In the meantime he had got everything ready for his journey, but had kept it secret from all but very few of his people. Nor would he take any of his own horses with him, but had four strong warhorses led up outside as if they belonged to the guests who intended to leave that night.

2006 And now nearly everyone was sitting at supper and God's vassal saw that this was the moment when he must go. It was raining as if it would never stop. (He had his cloak cut short once that night; it was so heavy he could hardly bear the weight.) When all was dark and everything was quiet, Archbishop Thomas got ready to go away secretly. He told no one, neither confidant nor clerk, relative nor friend, except three men who had worked for him before. The good baron took with him two white brethren: Robert of Cave, I have heard one of them called, and the other, brother Scaiman.[21] There was one squire, too, whom he did not want to leave behind him—Roger of Brai, a brown-haired, brave young man.[22] He told his plan to these two brothers, who had come to him from Sempringham,[23] and to his squire, who was in his confidence. They left the place at night by the north gate, where none of them were seen or challenged. Yet all the burgh gates were being watched (I cannot tell you why, but we can very well guess, considering the times). But the baron sent men to look at every gate, and this was the only one found without guard or gatekeeper.[24]

2031 Thomas the Archbishop was in no mood to linger; he had been told plainly that if he stayed till daylight he would be put in prison, and he did fear that this would happen. They went away under the stars and the cloak of darkness, commending themselves to God our Lord. (They travelled all night long till daybreak, and at dawn they would hide until the evening, with monks, with nuns, in the woods, to conceal themselves. They avoided taking the direct route—and at last they came to the sea.)

2041 Next day the king's messenger went three times before tierce[25] to hurry the Archbishop, to order him to come to court, but the man guarding the door would not let him in, saying that he must let him rest longer; eventually, however, he was so urgent that the secret could be kept no longer. Then the marshal, Sir William of Capes,[26] went to King Henry and asked his mercy for the Archbishop's men, to protect them against harm, because de Broc's men were their bitter enemies, and nearly all of them had gone away. King Henry then made Ranulf de Broc proclaim throughout Northampton that the Archbishop's men were to be allowed to depart freely in broad daylight, no one was to dare to touch any of them. Ranulf did this reluctantly, but he did not dare refuse.

2056 On the first night after Thomas had slipped away as he did, the second day,[27] he entered Lincoln, where he and his men stayed with Sir Jacob.[28] In order to keep hidden, he put on a brother's grey habit—now Thomas was Thomas no longer, but was called Christian. Before daybreak Saint Thomas went aboard a boat, taking Robert of Cave with him secretly; he passed straight under Lincoln bridge and made his way to the hermitage[29] in the direction of Sempringham. He stayed there in one room for a week or longer. Scaiman and Roger went by dry land; they arrived at Sempringham, where they stayed and got everything ready quietly for the Archbishop's journey, telling no one, high or low, what their plans were. They went from place to place at night, as they saw their chance. Anyone who saw the holy man sitting down to his meal without clerk or knight, whether friend or stranger, beside him (when Robert was away), with no seneschal or servant, no cook, no butler, would have felt tears of compassion trickling down his face.

CHAPTER FOUR

Exile

2076 THEY STAYED a long time at the hermitage, until the king thought they had crossed the sea, and then they set off, still travelling at night, to go to the coast. (All the places where they were to stay were arranged beforehand.[1]) They even went through Canterbury at night. The baron reached the sea, took ship at Sandwich, and landed late in the evening between Gravelines and Marck.[2] He could not travel on foot, as he tired very quickly. He was wearing a pair of big shoes, lent him by a brother, which he laced and knotted round his instep. Trying to hurry, he stumbled and fell on the shingle; then he got up and stood looking at his hands. After that they hired a mare for him, without a saddle, for that was all they could get at the time. All that its master had put on it was a halter made of hay. They had come across a lad on the beach and hired a horse from him for eightpence; when he went to fetch it, he was absent a long time, and they thought they would all be denounced or arrested. Then he brought this mare, and they put Christian up on it. They got him to ride two leagues, bareback, with just a folded cloak under him. Then they went together to Clairmarais by boat, and after that to St. Omer;[3] they did not want to delay. They took care to be well concealed when finding places to stay.

2101 The next thing that happened was that Sir Richard de Lucy arrived in St. Omer, on his way from St. James,[4] via Flanders. He heard the Archbishop spoken of, and went to see him. He would reconcile him, he said, to King Henry, if he would go back with him. But his efforts were useless; the Archbishop replied that he did not wish to go back because he could not possibly reconcile him, and he did not want to entrust his person into his hands like that; he meant, he said, to go straight to the Pope, and he would be entirely guided by his advice. This made Richard angry, and he answered arrogantly,

2112 'As you refuse to come to the king with me, then I now defy you, for myself and for my men.' Without a trace of pride or anger, the Archbishop said to him,

'You are my man, Richard, you owe me fealty.'

'I return my homage to you', Richard said.

'I did not lend it to you!' he retorted. 'But from now on you will certainly hold nothing from me.'

'I do not return to you', said Richard, 'either fief or holding, but see that in future you do not count on me for anything.'[5]

2121 Then the baron sent two abbots to the count,[6] asking for a safe conduct so that he could pass through Flanders, where he had landed because he had left England privately, on account of his lord the king, with whom he was at odds. The count replied that he would consider the matter; and that he was so rich[7] a man that he could well, he said, retain an Archbishop in the lands he possessed. When the Archbishop heard this answer, he discussed it with the bishop of Thérouanne,[8] and this man got him away by night. Thomas feared very much for his safety, hearing that reply; he paid particular attention to the count's words because the count was a cousin of King Henry's—they were like-minded men and very close friends. He told Bishop Milo what he thought. Milo had come that day to visit the Archbishop. When he left at night, in the dark evening, Thomas the Archbishop, who was such an intelligent man, went to see him on his way. He had the candles put out, so that he should not be noticed.

2141 'Put out those candles', he said to them; 'leave this departure to God.' And so he saved himself. They withdrew, and he mounted a big white horse which had been brought to him from this bishop's court—so he got away. He slipped away from his own men in the dark, by means of Bishop Milo, who got him away by night; he left Flanders and went to Soissons. Next day he sent a message back to his men, telling them he was going to Soissons, and they were to join him there.

2151 After this he enjoyed a stroke of excellent fortune, which many have subsequently thought was a miracle: Sir Henry of Pisa,[9] one of the cardinals, and King Louis had gone to Soissons from some other place, and they and Thomas recognised each other in the street. He told them about his situation and how he was in exile; Louis, the good king, was very distressed about it and expressed a wish to support him with all friendship. Sir Henry of Pisa too promised that he would do all he could to help him, and so he did, most faithfully.

2161 Then King Henry sent his messengers to Louis, King of France, at Compiègne, stating that in the agreement arranged between them when they had been made friends, which they had granted and promised to each other, it was declared that if any one of their vassals should leave their land and be recognised anywhere in the other's land, he should be at once arrested and detained, and returned without hindrance to his lord. The most important men in the kingdom came abroad: Gilbert Foliot formed part of the embassy—a well read man, a servant of Astaroth! (But the time was to come when he thought himself a fool for ever having said a word against the holy man. He went out from Sodom and followed in Lot's footsteps.) Richard of Ilchester[10] was another of the messengers; he was King Henry's confidential adviser, and was master and justiciar of the whole land. He brought two hawks to King Louis. (Now he goes by the right road; he has left the byways.) Another was William, the good Earl of Arundel,[11] a man of wisdom, valour and good breeding, quite free from any roughness of manner; but at this time he was contributing his gold to cast the calf; he did wrong, in trying to put Daniel into the pit. (He has gone to the saint's tomb for forgiveness.) They delivered their message competently, in well chosen phrases.

2187 'I do not know what you are talking about', King Louis said.

'My lord', they said, 'King Henry makes complaint to you, complaint of one of the most important men in all his land, who has fled out of England by night. Thomas the Archbishop has acted wrongly towards the king: he controlled the entire kingdom and received all its revenues for many years and days; he refuses to account for all that he has taken out of it, or to accept judgment. This has very much damaged his good name. And since he refuses to account to his lord for his lord's goods that he has had, and flees from his judgment, his departure seems to us to be nothing less than criminal. The king now requests you in all friendship, that he should find no refuge anywhere in your land.'

2201 'Archbishop Thomas', said the king, 'yes, indeed, I have seen him. He was that chancellor who served King Henry so well. He has driven him out of his realm, and still hates him so much that he is not to find shelter anywhere. A generous reward for such good service! Yes, indeed, I knew Archbishop Thomas very well. I tell you, by those holy relics I have been visiting, that France is free so that those who need refuge may find it here. He is most welcome; he will find protection here. If I knew where to go, I would go and meet him.' The Earl of Arundel said,

2211 'My lord King Louis, know that King Henry informs you through us that this man has been a deadly enemy to you: he has laid waste your lands, taken your castles, and it is he who has so often caused the king to act against you.'

2216 'My lord earl', said the king, 'I am perfectly sure that a man who served his lord so loyally would have served me well, if he had been my man. And if he conquered lands and castles for him, that is all the more reason why he ought to hold him dear.'

2221 'My lord', they said to the king, 'send to the Pope, for the love of our king, whom you ought to love dearly, and tell him not to listen to Thomas the Archbishop, who has stolen away like this, nor to support him or take him into his confidence; tell him not to give hearing or credit to his lies.' At that the king sent for brother Franc,[12] the almoner.

2226 'Quickly', he said, 'go to the Pope at once, do not delay. Tell him that if he wants any assistance from me, he must help the Archbishop, support him, make much of him, and not allow anyone or anything to persuade him otherwise.' (Brother Franc was a man who was high in the Pope's confidence, attached to his almonry and ready night and day to serve him; he was well known everywhere as such. At this period he was visiting King Louis.)

2236 The messengers left Compiègne, and brother Franc delivered his message very well; he repeated it to the Pope, who listened attentively. Archbishop Thomas travelled on until he reached Sens, where he found the Pope.[13] But the king had sent his envoys to the Pope—bishops, barons, and well known knights—before the friend of God reached Sens. (The Pope had at that time fled from Rome; he stayed at Sens for months, weeks and days.) The Archbishop who was master of York went there, and so did Guy le Roux,[14] and the bishop of Worcester, the Earl of Arundel, Richard of Ilchester, John of Oxford, the bishop of Exeter, Hugh de Gundeville,[15] and Hilary of Chichester. Reginald of St. Valéry[16] went too, and so did Henry Fitzgerald,[17] the king's close friend; also Gilbert Foliot, who was far from silent, and a good many others, both young and white-haired. All the same, one of the speakers made a fool of himself. The royal envoys stood before the Pope; some of them spoke well, many not so well. Some used Latin—correct Latin, some of them, and incorrect too: one man turned an impersonal verb into a personal one; singular and plural were all alike to him.[18] One of the prelates[19] spoke so bitterly that the Pope said to him,

2262 'Gently, *frater*, I will not have him insulted.' I have not got every word they said here beside me, but I will tell you what they requested, as far as I know it.

2266 'My lord', said the envoys to him, 'King Henry requests and beseeches you, as his most dear father, to send him two cardinals with full powers to bind and to loose, who cannot be opposed by any appeal; they should be so strong and so empowered that all that they shall do may stand firm, without the possibility of there being any opposition or appeal expressed before them. And if King Henry has in any way acted wrongly towards the Archbishop, let them put it right; if the Archbishop has offended him, let them amend, determine, and conclude the matter'. All this sounded marvellously upright, but there was not a word of sincerity in it all, nothing but deceit and great treachery. The king was rich, and he was also clever, indeed cunning, and he knew that cardinals are grasping Lombards, more anxious for wealth than a villein for newly-cleared land. The king has two dear friends, Redgold and Sir Silver; they can make a good man bad in a moment, or a brave man a coward.

2286 They did not succeed in deceiving the Pope. Like a wise man, he replied,

'No cardinal can have such power. Not one of them is going to obtain power of unreason by my means, nor do I intend to set anyone up in papal authority.'

2291 At the time that the king's envoys went there, Reginald the Archdeacon was living at Corbeil.[20] He went to Paris to meet the messengers and begged them affectionately to do him the honour of staying with him; he would be most grateful to them. He was, he said, of a good family in his own country, but had left it because of his Archbishop. If they would do him the honour he was asking, then Louis the good king (who had at that time made him abbot of Corbeil) would be the more friendly disposed towards him.

'We will not eat with you', they said, 'because of the king. He does not love you, and so would hold it against us.'

'You will not be able to get your business with the Pope done quickly', he said. 'If you stay with me at my expense, you will be able to avenge the king on one of his enemies'. After this they went on to Sens to the Pope.

2307 Since he had refused to do what they asked,[21] the Pope did grant them one thing: that Roger of York should be legate of the kingdom. The letters about this were written but never delivered. Reginald the Lombard was trusted at the court, and when he heard that this arrangement had been made, he went to the court secretly at night—for the king of England was much feared in the daytime, and he did not want any accusation brought against him. He said to the Pope,

2316 'Do not do this, my lord. If Roger of York gets the legation, he will depose all the prelates whom the king dislikes.' He managed to get the Pope to tear up all the letters that he had had written, and give them different ones.

2321 The king's envoys did all they could to gain their ends, but they could get no more. They mounted their horses and departed. Reginald of St. Valéry had friends in the country, otherwise they would have been roughly treated. They would not wait for their Archbishop, as they could not attack him in any quarter—he would soon tell the Pope things about them which would promptly prove an embarrassment to them; they could not defend themselves on all points.

2331 Within four days after this Saint Thomas arrived at Sens and went to his lodgings, for he was tired with travelling. He discussed with his clerks the question as to who should state his case. They did not deceive him—they all behaved very faint-heartedly. Not one of them would do it, however much he ordered or begged them to; none of them dared to make the speech, on account of King Henry. They would never, they said, have his friendship in all their lives. The Archbishop undertook it himself—God was his friend—and next day, when he had served Our Lord, he went to the Pope and fell at his feet.

2341 It is the custom that those who go into the Pope's presence offer at his feet some gift—gold or silver, rich plate or handsome ornament. The Archbishop took the king's chirograph in his two hands and stretched it out at the Pope's feet.

2346 'This is the reason why I have to endure exile. See, my lord, here it is. You should listen to it—these are the kind of laws that the king wants to establish in his kingdom, and he is trying to compel holy church to keep them, by force. But I will not give him my consent, against God. My lord, this is why I have come here, to show you this.' Then the Pope made him stand up and ordered that the laws be read out and listened to. The saint began to show point by point the aim towards which the king was moving by means of these laws. There was a cardinal present who was much attached to the king, called, I believe, William of Pavia.[22] (The king had got all the cardinals on his side, because he had given to them so liberally, and provided them with good reason to stand up for his case, both publicly and in private.) When the Archbishop started speaking and was explaining his case in very elegant Latin, this man kept contradicting him—he thought that the Archbishop had learnt his speech by heart, and that if he interrupted him, he would not be able to finish. Saint Thomas was a very intelligent man; the Holy Spirit was present in him—he took in all that this other man said and answered every word; he explained each point in good Latin. This man kept him discussing his case at least half the day. Then when he had answered his questions, he would come back to his own points like a Solomon, expounding his case with very fine reasoning. The debate between them lasted half a day at least, for this man opposed him point by point in his teeth.

2376 The Archbishop completed his excellent chain of reasoning; he demolished the laws by well-supported argument, by consistent logic and clearly-demonstrated proof; both laymen and clerks listened attentively to him, and the Pope took careful notice of all his points. Then the Pope at once made him sit down next to himself and bade him welcome over and over again; he deserved great gratitude, he said, for undertaking so heavy a burden as to defend holy church against an earthly king. He would assist him wherever reason would permit him to do so. Thomas the Archbishop thanked him repeatedly for his kind welcome and for doing him such honour. After this the Pope excommunicated the laws and anyone, whoever he might be, who should ever observe them; he confirmed this for ever upon anathema.

The Constitutions of Clarendon

2391 If you would like to hear these laws[23] that King Henry wanted to establish and set up in his kingdom and to make holy church observe and keep, you may learn them here; I shall tell no lies. Saint Thomas abominated them, and therefore everyone must do so.

2396 'If a dispute over a church were to arise, whether between laymen or between lettered men (between laymen: which of them was the advocate;[24] between clerks: which of them had been presented) the dispute should be heard and settled in the king's court.' This takes no notice of holy church's rights.

2401 'No one should grant away a church in the king's fief without the king's permission.' You can see for yourselves that the whole kingdom is his, it is his duty to govern it all, and by means of this law he could outwit everyone and bring all the churches into his gift.

2406 'Clerks should answer all accusations in the king's court, and after that be taken to the court of holy church, where the king's justice would be present at the proceedings. Men found guilty would be unfrocked and mutilated.' It is not right that a man should suffer twice for one offence.

2411 'No prelate or beneficed clerk should leave England without the king's permission, and even then he must also swear that he seeks no harm against the king or kingdom.' If this were put into operation, no powerless man would ever be able to obtain his rights. King Henry would hold St. Peter's powers.

2416 'Excommunicates should not give pledges so that holy church may correct them for their misdeeds, but only so as to be absolved of their chief sin.'[25] Most people would be set free to sin as much as they liked if it were not that the clergy restrained them.

2421 'No one, clerk or layman, should bring an accusation against any layman, except before the bishop; nor should he reply to it there unless he hears honest witnesses speak against him (always provided that the archdeacon does not lose his rights).' But according to this law, none of them would get anything by this. 'If this man be such that no one dares accuse him, then the bishop must inform the sheriff about it; he should establish the truth by means of 12 men who will swear it to the best of their knowledge.' So from now on, God is to make his complaint to St. Peter!

2431 'No one holding land of the king in chief, nor any of his officers, nor their lands, ought to be put under interdict or excommunication unless the king has been consulted, if he be in the country or the kingdom. If the king cannot be found in the country, the prelate must go to the justice and conclude the king's business in the king's court, and the prelate's in his.' A man who judges sins may as well confess them too!

2441 'The archdeacon must hear appeals in the first instance; thence they must go to the bishop, and then to the archbishop. If he cannot deal with them, the king must then have them concluded in God's court; and they must not leave his court without his permission.' That would set King Henry's court high indeed! since he has placed it above that of Rome. The whole of England would be deprived of divine justice; she would not be admitted amongst the 12 tribes if Moses were not the supreme judge.

2451 'If a clerk brings an action against a layman in order to convert a lay fee into land held as free alms, or if a layman wants to convert free alms land into a lay fee, the justice must obtain testimony from 12 men as to whether this fee should be held as free alms or as a lay fief. If both men acknowledge that they hold from one lord, clerk or layman, they must go to his court; but if they recognise two lordships to this fief, they must plead in King Henry's court. But the testimony shall not cause them any loss of seisin.' Neither clerk nor lay ought to allow this clause, for it could lead to the loss of holy church's rights, it could bring loss to laymen and clerks alike—the oaths of the 12 men could well deprive a lord of his fief and force him to abandon it to his vassal.

2466 'If anyone belonging to a castle, burgh, city or demesne manor of the king be accused before his prelates of any crime, and fails to appear voluntarily in answer to their lawful summons, this shall be reported to King Henry's officer; he, if he does not compel the man to make proper amends, must himself be disburdened by the king's mercy.[26] And after this the prelate may do justice on the accused man—previous to this, he was on no account to be excommunicated, but might properly be made to leave the church.'

2476 'All prelates and beneficed clergy of the country who hold lands and possessions of the king must hold of him in chief as barons; they must be present at his judgments like his other associates, until a question of death or dismemberment arises.' A clerk has no right to judge a layman, nor a layman a clerk. No one should hold free alms in chief of anyone but God. And if the king can set himself up as equal to God, then he can go and hunt all the saints out of heaven. I wonder what corner he would leave for God?

2486 'If any place in the kingdom became vacant—bishopric, priory, abbey or archbishopric—the king would seize its fiefs and estates; he would have its revenues and hold them in his leashes until the place should be provided with a pastor.' I have been to several places that had been seized by the king—no guests or poor people were made welcome there. I myself was turned away from the door by the porter—from what he said, I gathered that charity was not at home. The king took away everything except the barest necessities. Monk and cook and servant, squire, and serving lad, they all received their exact ration of bread, for the king's servants were in the house. And they, when they left, caused such destruction that you would not have been able to find any provisions, no, not the least little capon. The king is doing wrong in this towards God and towards the place in question; also towards the barons whose fathers established the church. They are performing the full service due from the fief, yet he takes their alms and puts it into his treasury, whereas it ought to go to the poor and to good uses. 'When the king shall decide to give the church a pastor'—for everything must go according to his wishes—'he will send for three beneficed clergy of the church and will assemble in his chapel such prelates and barons as he shall think fit.' Now, if one needed to take thought for the church according to God, learning and nobility ought to be kept out, for wisdom would try to outwit the barons, valour and nobility would use their strength against the prelates —in that kind of situation, simony can exalt a man of little worth. 'The elected man must do immediate homage to the king, fealty and liege homage, as to his liege lord, for his limbs and for his earthly honour.' Thus the Saviour's servants would have to do homage, although if it were not for the crosier none of them would ever have done it.

2521 'If any man attempts forcibly to deprive prelates of their rights, the king will do them justice regarding both that man and any other. If it should happen that anyone should be so obstinately opposed to the king as to prevent him from exercising his rights, then the prelates shall do justice to this man with regard to the king.' It is the duty of the king to defend holy church and the clergy; they ought not to bear arms or take part in great wars; their duty, whoever they may be, is to serve God night and day, not to harass the king's enemies for him, nor for this reason to part Frenchman or Welshman from God.

2531 'If anyone's goods are forfeit to King Henry, they are not to be stored in any cemetery or church after the justice has been there.'[27] I am sure that if any thief or robber or such ill-fated man went there, the church and cemetery would be a shield against him.

2536 'All pleas of debt, under pledge of faith or not, should be heard in the king's court.' It would not be right for me to plead in a lay court on a criminal matter; clerks shall have their own courts and their own law for debt and for other questions, as do all those who live and are provided for by almsgiving.

2541 'No villein's son shall ever be ordained without the consent of the lord on whose land he was born.' And God has called us all to his service! Better an intelligent and valiant man whose father was a villein than a gently born coward and outcast![28]

2546 Such were the clauses of King Henry's laws. I tell you truly, Alexander the good Pope excommunicated them, as Saint Thomas did too, and anyone who should in future keep them. The law in them is very convenient for wild fools and criminals; every man of faith ought to oppose it, for it is utterly displeasing to the heavenly king. How high he has exalted his champion, who undertook the battle to bring down this arrogance!

2556 After the Archbishop had stayed at Sens over a month in attendance on the Pope, the latter sent him to Pontigny, to the white monks who lived there, and Guichard, the abbot, who obtained for him all that he needed.[29]

Henry's Anger at Thomas's Flight

2561 This has been a very long digression, but I did not want to misrepresent the facts in any way. Now I must return to my narrative, and go back to the point where the saint had fled from Northampton. I shall tell you what the king did about this.

2566 When King Henry heard that the Archbishop had fled, he was furious, and so were his advisers. They had all the ports watched night and day so that he would be unable to escape, in a full boat or an empty one. But this was useless, for God had led him out of the country. When they could not find him anywhere in England (nor will they be able to, unless they go and look for him at Sens), the king gave up all self restraint and let his anger rage—he attacked Saint Thomas's relatives and had every one of them driven out of his land. He drove them all out, men and women, beneficed clerks, citizens, knights, with their sons and daughters, their babes in arms; he seized everything into his own hands, lands and churches, live-stock and dead stock, corn, rents, money. He even seized the whole archbishopric, rents, fiefs, and all its wealth, and gave it in charge to Ranulf de Broc, who collected all its income for the king's use. The saint could not get a single halfpenny of it all. No recovery could the holy man obtain of any of it; not one of all his clerks dared go there; none of his people could get anything there to eat or drink. Instead, the king had them all driven out of the country, he took it all to his own use, down to the last penny. And so Saint Thomas's kinsfolk were all driven away; they went, sad and weary, into another country, carrying their children and their clothes and cloaks. How truly does the villein say 'The greater the height, the further the fall.' They used to be rich, but now not one of them looks properly fed.

2596 The Archbishop was sitting at his meal one day, when his marshal came to tell him the news, that the king had had his entire family exiled, and within three days there would be more than a hundred of them; he begged him for God's sake not to let it upset him.

2601 'William', he said to him, 'if I were to see my servants cut to pieces for this cause, and my kinsmen flayed, my sisters and nephews, it would not dismay me, for I would know for certain that they were saved by the divine pity.' The devil could get no access to him by any path—he had had him evicted from great wealth and from his own country; now he was trying to distress him through his flesh and blood, but he could not discourage him by any affliction. No one can tell you all the suffering he endured. When the saint saw his own people coming towards him as fugitives, the tiny children hanging on their mothers' breasts, and he knew that the king had proscribed both him and his, he would rather have died, so keen was his grief. But he took comfort in God and the divine scriptures. He thought of Abraham: when God ordered him to leave his own country, the baron went, leaving all his friends; he took his wife with him, and the king stole her because she was so beautiful; God brought her safely back to him and greatly exalted him. He remembered Joseph, whose nine brothers sold him for money and told their father that a wild beast had eaten him; afterwards he was more than emperor in Egypt and preserved his relatives from the bitter famine. He reminded himself too of what had happened to the infant Jesus, whom the heavenly angel sent into Egypt for fear of Herod; and Herod then had all the two-year-old children beheaded, for he thought he could kill God—but he did not manage to find the Deity amongst the children. He took great courage from such examples, but all the same it distressed him very much that his relatives should be exiled for his sake, since he did not possess great fiefs or other inheritances which he might have been able to give them, and so was all the more at a loss. None the less, things did not go too badly for him during his exile, as King Louis paid all his expenses and found all that was needed, both for him and for his people. The French barons helped him very much too, and so he was able to assist his kinsfolk who came to him.

Henry Forbids Communication with Rome

2641 When King Henry heard that the Pope was sending out letters summoning the bishops, he assembled his council at Clarendon. Here he tried to make the bishops swear that none of them would ever cross the sea for any appeal, that they would never obey Pope Alexander in anything, nor ever do anything he might order, nor ever in future receive any letter from him; that they would never assist Thomas nor his people in any way. They did not swear to this, but assented to it. The laymen were made to swear to it all. Truly,

Roger had so much money that Rome had shifted to York! With Sir Gold on his side, he had Rome in his pocket. England is fenced in by the sea and the winds, so that if there is but a little storm, she fears neither God nor his saints. Furthermore, the king ordered and proclaimed that if there were any clerk in all his land so rash as to appeal to Rome, all his goods should at once be seized to King Henry's use, and he should be imprisoned like a man of ill fame. All men then made their appeals to the king and pleaded in his court, where there was never a whisper of law. Poor clerks were treated there quite contrary to all law, for the rich man could always sway the church as he wished. I can bear faithful witness to what I both hear and see. St. Peter's Pence were withheld, too, and were taken and handed in to the Exchequer. The sea coasts were watched and guarded: if anyone were to be discovered bringing a letter from Rome, he would at once be arrested and hanged. A good many did come from there none the less, at Pope Alexander's orders; they travelled very secretly and brought letters of warning to such prelates as had erred seriously, or of suspension, or of excommunication.

2676 After this, Saint Thomas sent for his bishops one after another. Not one would go to him except Roger, the earl's son;[30] he crossed the sea at once, without the sheriff's permission; he disgraced neither his primate nor holy church. Seven years he was in exile; greatly did he lend at interest.

2681 Listen now to the writs which the king sent to the sheriffs of the country. Walter of Grimsby took them (the writ mentions him by name), and Wimer the chaplain who went with him.[31] I will tell you briefly what it said: if anyone brought a letter into the country from the Pope, or one sent by Archbishop Thomas, forbidding or prohibiting Christianity, he must be arrested at once and kept until King Henry should order his pleasure concerning him. If a clerk, monk, canon or lay brother were to cross the sea, he must take with him a letter about it from the justice; anyone wanting to return to England must carry the king's letter saying that he wished him to go there, otherwise he would be arrested and imprisoned. No one must keep or observe any order sent by the Pope or by Archbishop Thomas, nor must anyone bring any of their orders into the country. If anyone encountered a man, clerk or lay, carrying such a letter, the man must at once be arrested and imprisoned. If the Pope or the Archbishop put anyone under an interdict and an abbot or bishop gave effect to the sentence, then, clerk or layman, he must flee the country and take all his kinsfolk with him, not leaving one of them behind. They would retain none of their possessions, the king would take it all. Clerks who owned estates and possessions should be summoned three times in each county; if they wished to return to their estates or their houses they must return within three lunar months, or else live the rest of their lives in poverty—the king would have all their goods down to the last penny. The reason he had this proclamation made was that Saint Thomas's clerks were afraid to go back, and he hoped by means of this summons to prevent them from returning and to make them exiles and outlaws for ever. The bishops of London and of Norwich should be summoned at law, the writ demanded, before justices chosen by the king, because they had put Earl Hugh under an interdict,[32] contrary to the decrees that the king had established in the realm. You see what bitter grief, what torture and death, holy mother church suffered at that time! not daring to exercise her law or do her justice; had she done so, vengeance would have been taken. The son gave his head for his mother's rights.

2726 There was another writ which I will tell you about: in it the king commanded that all the people of England should collect Peter's Pence and keep it faithfully until he should give further orders. The English have this great advantage in their country, which was first begun by King Cnut,[33] the Dane—this penny is taken annually from every house which possesses more than five shillings' worth of livestock. (In some places it is

30 pence.) Traditionally, the Pope received this penny and thus greatly relieved the English, as it was not necessary to send them away from home because of sin; they could do all their penance at their own firesides. But now the king took it and had it locked away. To my mind the king was quite right to take it—was he not pope, legate and archbishop? If archbishop or pope put his lands under interdict, the king absolved them without cross or stole. Holy church could show no right compared with his.

Coronation of the Young King

2746 At this time King Henry had his son Henry sworn as king, and had him crowned.[34] Archbishop Roger did not want to refuse him; he crowned him king. He ought never to have thought of doing it, for it is always Canterbury's duty to consecrate kings. Two other bishops acted jointly with the Archbishop—Gilbert Foliot of the city of London and Jocelin of Salisbury. Others were present, whose names I omit; the burden was on these three and the work was done by them. These three wicked men anointed the child—may God increase his years, his virtue and his honour! But it did not belong to them to do it, they acted like thieves, although the words of the sacrament are not any the worse, nor is he any the less consecrated. God grant him his love! Without any reason they borrowed another's powers with which to do another's task—but they have paid for it dearly. They were summoned for it to Rome, but did not go, and the Pope cut them off from their calling. Out of fear of the king, they threw God aside. Oh God, how sad it is when prelates fail to exercise their calling! The light that enlightens the world is hidden—they are the stinking salt that rots the spirit[35]—dumb dogs that do not bark, they lie contentedly under the bench,[36] they welcome the thieves and join them in their crime.

2771 These three adhered unhesitatingly and completely to the king; for God they would do nothing, nothing at all. They were united in a false trinity, these three men, and as far as truth was concerned, they kept absolute silence. They tried to turn the customs into law. They made no attempt to correct their lord, but instead got him to attack holy church. They went to endless trouble to examine documents to see if they could find any point that might possibly support the king's case. They stuck together closer than uncle and nephew, and kept writing to Saint Thomas, telling him that he was wrong to be so harsh towards the king, for the king is lord and head of the churches, and the churches are constructed out of royal fiefs. Prelates ought undoubtedly to obey kings; kings ought certainly to be allowed to maintain their customs—as no one ever made their ancestors do away with them, they need not abandon them now, for the sake of anyone at present alive. It was the duty of both clerks and laymen to be infinitely patient towards their lords.

2791 They sent this sort of letter across the sea to the holy man, and several more about which I am not informed, in the hope of pleasing the king and of showing how clever they were. Thomas wrote his answers and had them taken to them, to destroy theirs and to establish his case. The saint replied to their letters with humility and supported everything he said from the scriptures; not one of the lot of them could gainsay him over any point. Indeed, the Holy Spirit dwelt within him; it spoke through him and by it he was made strong. It is very right to obey earthly lords in earthly matters, but if they attempt to take anything from holy church, this must not be allowed. And if one were to spare them, being reluctant to strike at them, yet when God should in due course will it, they would not be able to escape. Prelates are God's servants, the king must cherish them—and they are the heads of kings, the king must give way to them. God is the prelates' head, and they ought to stretch out their necks, ready for death, in order to maintain his law—God endured death on the cross to free his church. Kings hold from God, from holy mother church; they owe honour and service to her and to hers, for from her they have received both law and the crown. She and all her people ought most certainly to have that freedom which Our Lord won for her by his death. And those good ancestors who made the churches, who first established them out of their own funds, and with their own almsgiving prospered and endowed them, they freed them from these and from all other customs; they never stretched out a single finger afterwards towards anything. For any person making a grant in alms must free it entirely, and must maintain and defend it in everything and against everyone; he has no right to retain the lordship over it, or anything else, for if he does what he likes with it, it is not alms. If he has given it to God, he cannot take it back again. And when the king, whose duty it is to defend and support holy church in every way, makes an attack on her, the bishops ought to rebuke him very strongly indeed; they ought not to give heed to his will in any respect. But they are like reeds that dare not stand up to the storm. Barons and knights, sergeants and vassals, who hold nothing of anyone but their ancestral fiefs, often do battle for their mortal lords and suffer great injuries, death, wounds and pain, because they do not want to be thought disloyal. Much more ought prelates to fight all those who try to oppose holy church, for they sit in high places, mighty, powerful, well loved, at God's table. God raises the sons of the very lowest-born men till they are given bishoprics or much higher posts. Prelates ought to be the most spiritual of men and never for any reason stumble from their position. Those who come down from the mountain and dwell in the valley are rings of gold set in pigs' snouts.[37] They are not God's servants, they are Baal's.

CHAPTER FIVE

Letters

2846 NOW I WILL LEAVE this topic and tell you of the letters that the good baron sent to the king and to the bishops, so that they might keep the peace of holy church; and give you a report of those that they wrote back to him.[1]

2851 'To the noble English king, Henry, Count of Anjou, Duke of Normandy and of Aquitaine, his lord and friend: Thomas the Archbishop, who formerly served him but now is his in God—greetings, and may he turn from and amend all the wrongs he has done.

2856 'I have waited in the hope that God might visit you, so that you would decide to leave your evil course and remove all your wicked advisers from about you—they, I fear, will sink you so deep that you will never manage to climb back up again. Till now I have endured everything and kept silent, hoping that someone would say to me, "The king who was dead and lost, your son and lord, is found and restored to life again. He had been deceived by wicked men's advice; now he has come to do right to holy church. He has opposed holy church for a long time, but from now on he will seek her deliverance. God's pity has led him to amend his way." Daily we pray to God for you in the sacrament, that by his pity he may set you in the right way.

2871 'I say this because you have sent me, whose duty it is under God to protect the kingdom's church and to remove wrongdoing, into exile, and made me leave the country, ill-treating holy church and her appointed people. I have borne it patiently, for I could not amend it. It grieves me deeply that you have behaved so wrongly towards holy mother church and her appointed servants, for I share in the offence by failing to do justice upon it. A man who is justice and judge, and who takes it lightheartedly, is equally guilty with the sinners. Holy scripture says and bears witness that he who consents to an offence is a party to it—all the more then, one who should and could but does not punish it. For obviously a man who refuses to make a stand against open folly, shares in the wrongdoing. I would wish, king, if I could, to correct you fully, and that is why I have had my letters sent to you so often.

2888 'A little burgh cannot bring down the honour of the kingdom; no more must you, king, reduce or alter the rights of holy church by any affliction. Right judgments must come from the priests. Whatever kind of man the bishop may be whom God has established—even should he be seen to fall as a human into great sin—as long as he desires to maintain religion and his order, earthly power has no right to cause his downfall. A religious prince, anxious to love righteousness, must build and raise new churches, must restore and build up those that have fallen, and must honour God's priests and the clerks and always defend them against attack. You ought to consider the good prince Constantine:[2] when clerks were brought before him and accused, he let them all be. "No one but the Lord God," he said, "can condemn you; you cannot be judged by a secular prince." As holy writ and the doctors demonstrate, God orders the apostles,[3] and none of their successors or of all those who labour in Our Lord's field should ever be ejected or expelled from their holding, for they are the servants and the dispensers[4] of Jesus Christ. Priests are masters, fathers and pastors in the law to all who live in the Christian faith. God hates the man who tries to subjugate his father; one who beats his master lives quite contrary to law—all the more then if he attacks the bearer of the iron collar and the rod.[5] If you are a good Christian and wish to keep your faith—and we heartily wish and believe that this is so—I must call you son, not bishop, of the church. It is not for you to teach or guide the priests—you must follow them, and it is their duty to lead the way.

2921 'You have your own privileges, your laws, your power; do not take anything from the divine order against its will. If, through bad advice, you have sinned against God, then stoop, stoop at once into humility, lest God draw his bow against you! If you do not repent promptly you will find that he has already taken aim. Whatever those traitors to God and to yourself may say, it will be no disgrace to you but a very great honour if you will utterly humble yourself before that mighty lord who brings down the proud and sets the humble in the high seat. Kings and princes ought indeed to fear him. He is able to revenge himself upon all men; who can stand against him?

2932 'You should remember, king, and keep well in mind what your circumstances were when God first found you, and how he has advanced you, increased and enriched you, and established your reign. All men envy you this, your enemies and your friends alike. God has chosen you, as all men, great and small, acknowledge—what recompense will you make for all the benefits he has conferred upon you? Will you destroy his churches and hunt out his clerks, counselled as you are by the wicked men who surround you, who make you wage war upon God and holy church?

2941 'Ordained men are the men to whom God speaks—"He that despises you, despises me,"[6] says he who never stumbles; "he that hates you, hates me and rebels against me; he that strikes you, strikes me, in the eye, in the very pupil of the eye". God hates any man who does harm to clerks, and punishes him. If you had given all the world to the poor, if you had taken the cross and followed Jesus Christ, you would not have repaid to God what he has done for you. Saul, chosen of God, perished with all his household and all his kin because he turned from God. The king Uzziah,[7] famous for his many victories over his enemies, became immoderately proud and puffed up because of his success; he gave no thanks to God, whose help had gained him everything; he presumed in his insolence to undertake the priests' office and was so rash as to carry the holy incense in the temple. God was angered, and struck him with leprosy. The priests of God there appointed flung him out of the temple. He never recovered but was blemished and leprous all the days of his life.

2961 'Fair king, if you will only look at what has been written, you will see that there have been many kings thus chosen by God, and that when he had advanced them in the world and cherished them, they have exercised their calling wrongly, against God—and he has brought them to nothing and to poverty again. Ahaz[8] was one who usurped God's work: he burned incense with the bishops *in domo domini.* He was a king and wanted to be a bishop as well. God was angry and covered him with leprosy; he was marked and spotted. It was his pride that destroyed him. The ark of God was put upon a cart and covered over; the oxen jibbed and the cart almost fell—Uzza[9] put his hand to it, to stop it falling, and God's wrath struck him down and killed him there and then, for this was the priests' task. How easy and pleasant it is, king, to learn by another man's mistakes! You must often have heard this saying. Ordained men, king, have holy church in charge; God never gave her to the powers of this world. All believers are under her; she has the lordship. Leave the rights of others alone, and all that belongs to others. Do not dispute with God what he has founded. It is from God that you have your power and your crown—you do not receive it secularly from any prince or law, for consecration and ordaining belong to prelates. Secular law must serve ecclesiastical laws. None but clerks must carry on pleas of the church, nor must secular law prevail over that of the church. It is the custom that Christian kings should obey holy church. The layman must not tread down the clerk but must hold him dear.

2991 'There are two things in this world by which it is ruled—the holy power of kings and of bishops. When all the world shall be gathered for judgment, then the prelates will answer for the crowned kings, so much the greater and heavier is their burden. Many bishops in times past have excommunicated kings and emperors and expelled them from the church: Pope Innocent made the Emperor Arcadius leave the church,[10] he would not refrain for his sake, because he had allowed St. Chrysostome to be exiled.[11] And indeed St. Ambrose the Bishop excommunicated the Emperor Theodosius[12] and cut him off from the church for a different fault which seemed much less; but in the end he made worthy amends for it, received absolution and was reconciled to God. David, prophet and king, lay with another man's wife, and had her lord, his good knight, killed. God sent Nathan to rebuke him, and he was not ashamed to humble himself at Nathan's feet and to pray for mercy. And because he begged for mercy, God granted him grace; he found that he was good, humble, and penitent.

3013 'King, you should always follow that good king's example—turn back to God, put down your grievous burden. You have done many other wrongs that I do not at present mention.

3016 'My lord king, I have written this to you for the time being (and you have done much else that is wrong, of which I have not told you), to find out whether you will condemn your sin. If only someone would say to me, "Your son, who was dead, is alive again"! How glad I would be if God were to fill you with his spirit. And if you refuse to listen to me or to grant what I ask—I who pray regularly for you to God before God's body—I will pray to God that he make haste to avenge all the injuries, the evils and the very great wickedness which you and yours commit and refuse to abandon. Truly, I will cry to the Lord of might, "Avenge, oh God, your people's spilt blood, and their innumerable afflictions! The pride of your enemies, who hate you and yours, has grown so great that I can no longer keep silence". Whoever may perform the work, king, it is at your hands that it will be required, for the man who starts the fire is the one who does the damage. If you do not let the clerks and holy church alone, God will take swift vengeance; he has already picked up his rod. It is now time he should begin the judgment in equity. For he well knows how to take the spirit from princes, he is able to abase kings, no one can flee from him. May God's grace avail to win your salvation. If you will repent quickly in true humility, you will gain salvation. May you always abide in it!'

Thomas Writes to Henry Again

3041 The Archbishop sent the following letter, with no greeting, to the king at Chinon.[13] He requested him very reasonably that he would allow him to return in peace to his house, and that he would give and grant possession of it to his mother church, both to him and to his people. If you would like to listen, I will soon tell you what was set down and written in this letter:[14]

3048 'My lord king', he said to him, 'I have earnestly longed to see you once and to speak with you face to face. I have longed for it for my own sake, and even more for yours. For my sake? If you were to see me, you would, I think, recollect my loyal and faithful service to you (so help me God in the day of dreadful terror, when he shall render to each man according to his deeds), and you would be sorry for me, a beggar in a foreign kingdom.

'Although, God be thanked, I am well provided for. And the apostle Paul has greatly strengthened me, for I have found in his epistles that all who desire to live righteously in God must suffer torment and distress. David the psalmist tells us too that he had never yet seen a man who lived loyally, forsaken, nor his offspring begging bread.

3066 'There are three reasons, which I will tell you, why I have longed to talk with you for your sake: you are my lord, it is my duty and my wish to counsel you; you are my king, I must therefore love you dearly; you are my son in

God, and so I must correct you. For you see how a father corrects his child, by kind words, and by harsh and biting ones, very often beating him with a cutting rod, so as to bring him back to goodness when he sees him doing wrong, either by his reproaches or by the harsh rod.

3076 'It was God's grace that anointed and crowned you, therefore you ought to strive hard and control yourself and base your whole life on right living, so that you may give a good example to others, for everyone watches to see what you do. There are some to whom you must be kind and gentle, because you are anointed and consecrated; to many you must be harsh, because you bear the sword that was given you in holy church so that you might cut down and conquer the enemies of God. When kings are anointed, as you well know, they receive the unction in three places: on the head, the breast and the arms, because they must possess in themselves great glory, knowledge, and might. It is your duty to apply that glory, wisdom and strength to good ends. You should consider those kings of ancient times who would not keep God's commandments: Nebuchadnezzar, and Solomon the baron, and Saul, they did indeed find God bitter to them, for he took all this away from them because they refused to love him. Hezekiah and David and many another, after they had behaved wrongly towards God their creator, earnestly humbled themselves and sorrowed and repented in their hearts. Then the grace of the most high king lavished glory, intelligence and valour upon them.

3102 'God founded holy church and established her and with his own blood freed and delivered her; for her he was spat at and beaten and endured death. He left his example for us all, so that we may follow in the way he went. For anyone who desires to share in the glory of heaven must be martyred in his body for the love of God, must put aside the body's will and all its comforts. As St. Paul said, "We must die for God, if we want to live with him, and suffer death for his sake". Holy church consists of two kinds of persons: it is made up of the people and the clergy; it rightly forms a unity in this division. The care of it under God belongs to the prelates, and is to be carried on and performed for the salvation of souls. And, as I well know, God said to St. Peter and to the clerks, "You are Peter, and on this rock I will make my church, I will build my house, and by means of it I will shatter the gates of hell". It is clerks who have this power, not laymen. Kings and other barons belong to the people; they have laymen subject to them and under their guardianship, also the secular laws and the power of which they stand possessed. But it is their duty to order everything in their charge so that holy church may be in unity and peace.

3126 'What is more, kings derive their power from holy church; she on the other hand does not take hers from any of your kings, but only from God her spouse who won it for her. Therefore you have no power to order prelates to exercise or to abstain from exercising ecclesiastical justice. It is not right that you should forbid or command prelates to absolve this man or condemn that, nor to haul or bring ordained clerks, not even one, to your judgments or before secular law, nor to start proceedings against any one of our churches, or about tithes. You have no right to forbid prelates to carry on their pleas, whether of transgression, of faith, of crime, or of false oaths—nor any right to the customs, usages and pleas that your ancestor maintained in years gone by.[15] Our Lord God said "Keep my laws"; and again the prophet said "Woe be to you who establish laws of wickedness and who put in writing wrongs and injuries, and to you who oppress God's poor and do violence to humble folk".[16]

3146 'Accept, my lord, the advice and the warning of a man who is sincerely faithful to you; receive your archbishop's admonition; listen to your father's kind rebuke. Hold no further communication with schismatics,[17] for it is known throughout almost all the world that you have done very great honour to the Pope and that you have cared for and upheld the church of Rome. The Pope and holy church have loved you. They have, with reason, done for you what you have asked. My lord, if you desire your soul's salvation, do not for any reason take from holy church anything that is hers; do not act unlawfully; allow holy church to enjoy all her liberties, as she does in all foreign kingdoms. You ought to call to mind the declaration which you offered on the altar when you were anointed, and the vow that you made to God in his house—you gave your protection to his bride and granted her her complete freedom. My lord, re-establish the holy mother church of Holy Trinity, from which you received your crown and kingship, in that dignity, in that condition and completeness, that she had in your ancestors' time and in antiquity. Give back to our clerks and laymen, re-establish completely, all her possessions and her other charges, both towns and castles, fiefs and manors, which you have seized and granted away at your pleasure. Allow us to return in peace, freely, and we will serve you loyally as our king and as our lord, as far as it is proper for us to do. Know for certain that if you do not do this, you will feel God's vengeance.'

From the English Clergy to Thomas

3181 The bishop of London sent a letter across the sea to Saint Thomas, but he concealed his name and drew it up in the name of the bishops of the country and the other beneficed clergy, but without naming any of them. He sent him love, submission, and greetings:[18]

3186 'Father, the kingdom was very gravely disturbed by your sudden departure from it, but we hoped that by means of your humility and your wisdom it would be restored through Almighty God's grace to its previous peaceful condition. At first we were able to take comfort and be glad when we heard the news told all over the kingdom that you were beyond the sea and did not mean to proceed against the king nor raise yourself up against him, nor to seek any harm or contrivance against the kingdom; but that you desired instead, of your own wish, to bear the burden of poverty, to devote yourself constantly to prayer and study, to make amends for what had been done wrong and for the loss of time past, in watching, in tears, and in much fasting, that you might win the love of the high king. Such works as these were the right ones to restore peace. We thought that by these means you would succeed in recovering the king's grace, that he would lay aside his anger and forgive you, forgetting the wrongs you had done him—you went away without his leave, and crossed the sea. Even those who loved you and wanted to support you were able to get access to the king and to talk to him, and when they asked him that you and he should be reconciled and peace and amity be established between you, he would at that time listen to them kindly.

3211 'Now we have heard very different news, which has moved us deeply, for you have sent a letter to the king that bears no greeting, you have not sought for or asked his forgiveness. We cannot perceive in a letter like this any evidence of friendship—and now you have threatened to excommunicate him. If you do this, as you have said you will, none of the disturbances and trouble in the country will ever be restored to love and concord; on the contrary, your action will produce hatreds that will last for ever, that no living man will be able to appease.

3221 'When a wise man embarks on something, he ought to think out thoroughly whether or not he will be able to finish it—you ought to demonstrate your excellent intelligence in this way, and consider whether you will be able to bring what you have begun to the end at which you are aiming. Your extreme audacity in threatening him as you have done has banished the good hope we had, for we do not see any means whereby you can be reconciled. You have marched upon him with your sword drawn, so that there are now no grounds upon which anyone might intercede for you. We therefore advise you sincerely and affectionately: do not commit one wrong after another, lest worse trouble develop. Commend your case to God the Creator, put a stop to your threats, show patience to your lord; your humility will soften his feelings towards you. This is the way for you to win his love and affection; you have gained nothing by your threats and would be able to win much more by humility. And it would become you better to endure poverty voluntarily than to hold great honours of him in rapacious greed.[19]

3241 'Everyone knows what remarkable honour he has done you—he raised you from the little that you were when he found you, and placed you very high; he gave you charge of the whole realm, so that anyone you looked on kindly thought himself lucky. He brought you from almost nothing to greatness, and piled honours upon you. Against the wishes and advice of his mother,[20] against the wishes of the whole kingdom, which was deeply displeased, and in spite of the bitter sighs of holy church, he succeeded in giving you the honour which you now hold. He supposed that you would not wish to thwart him, but would take thought for the kingdom and see to its wellbeing in every way. You are trying to bring down the man to whom you owe counsel—this is an evil way to thank him for the benefits he has done you. You have given everyone the right to speak ill of you. Do not throw away your reputation and your honour; overcome your lord the king by love. If you do not trust the advice that so many people give you, pay attention to the Pope's advice and affection, to the church of Rome, the unshakeable.

3261 'It is essential to make it quite clear to you that you must not do anything which might throw holy church into still greater distress (and she has been in tears and sorrow for many a day) and which would have to be paid for by men who were in no way to blame but would have to bear the brunt of another man's wrongdoing. What will you find to say if the king, to whom the kingdom belongs and who controls both the clergy and the people, should withdraw from the Pope on account of your provocations and never afterwards be subject to him? (For it is out of affection for you that he is opposing the king.) Look how people beg him to do this, what gifts they offer him! But however much they promise, he has no intention of doing this, he stands as firm as a rock against the gale. But I do fear, my lord, that this man who is unmoved and untempted by the whole world, may yet change of himself, although God forbid that he should! But if this were to come about because of you, it would be for you to grieve, tears ought to cover your face. And therefore take careful thought, so that harm does not come to the Pope, and great damage be not done to the church of Rome and to you. But your clever clerks are reluctant to allow it; they urge you to try all that you can do and to demonstrate your power to the king and his people—a power that the wrongdoer ought to fear, and that the man who will not amend ought to dread.

3286 'We do not say that the king has not made mistakes and done wrong, but he is always prepared to put matters right. It is his duty to preserve peace in the realm, that is why God set him there, and so that he may the better maintain peace in the country he wishes to have the customs and laws which are established in the kingdom. Perhaps there has been trouble between you and the king, but the Pope has often reasoned with him about it, the prelates of the realm have admonished him; if, he says, he has in any way damaged any church or incumbent, he will accept the judgment of his kingdom's church. He is ready to do right, and more, if anyone asks him; if he acts wrongly towards God, he is glad to be told of it. Since, then, he humbles himself towards holy church and God, there is no law, no canon, nothing, which may put him under interdict, no ecclesiastical sword which may wound or kill him. Put up your sword, follow good judgment. We all ask you: do not overreach yourself, do not kill for the sake of a hasty decision, take care of the flock that is under you, see that it enjoys safety and peace.

3306 'One thing you have done that grieves us very much: you have excommunicated the bishop of Salisbury, and his dean as well.[21] But it is proper to have thorough knowledge of a case, to hear it and deal with it, before pronouncing sentence. And in order that you may not do the same to the king and the kingdom, to the churches and parishes entrusted to us, that you may not illegally and wrongfully excommunicate them, to the injury of the Pope and, I believe, of yourself, we make appeal, for a remedy and shelter in this disorder. We appoint Ascension Day as the appeal day. But we all ask you; think better of it, do not make the journey, do not put yourself to such trouble or your sons to such expense. We desire your salvation in Our Lord God.'

Thomas's Answer

3321 Saint Thomas wrote back at once to the bishop of London. Instead of a greeting, there were friendly words wishing that he might so pass through temporal good things that he lose not the joy of the spirit.[22]

3326 'It is most extraordinary that an intelligent, well-educated man, one who has adopted the holy dress of a religious order, should put the fear of God so far from him, should act against truth and should scheme worse things yet, trying to bring down holy church and those who are appointed therein. Holy church can batter down the gates of hell—anyone trying to make her stumble is stupid indeed; he is like a man trying to pull down a mountain with a rope. Neither anger nor personal emnity should cause anyone to insult a bishop, nor his brother in the Lord God's work. But I see from your letter that I cannot gather grapes from thorns, or figs from briars. Anyone listening to it would think it was like a scorpion at the head and tail—one end welcoming, the other trying to sting. You started by offering obedience and submission; then you escape from this by making an appeal. Your "yes" turns negative fast enough. "Is it not with me", the apostle Paul said, "*yes, yes* and *no, no?*"[23] An honest man's mouth should express only the one or the other. God, we know, gave his disciples power to tread on snakes and scorpions.[24] Ezekiel dwells still among wicked men![25] What kind of remedy is your appeal to you? You follow

God, so you say, but we see no sign of it. Jesus Christ gave us a remedy for all our ills–obedience. He himself was an example of it, for he was obedient to God, creator of all things, until he died on the holy cross. What you call a remedy involves no little injury.

3356 'Do you imagine that the Pope will support you, when you ask to be allowed to disobey your master? You have asked him twice, and he has refused to listen to you, for it is his duty to support authority and bear the burden of seeing that holy obedience is everywhere upheld. First of all you made him this request by word of mouth, and then you made this wicked suggestion by letter–he is firmer than the rock set on a living foundation, he is the vicar of St. Peter, you know that he is no weathercock. He is not a man to be softened or moved to recklessness by gifts, presents or prayers. But you must be sure to attack him for the third time, so that at the third assault he may win the complete victory.

3368 'And you have fixed the appeal nearly a year away, so as to distress me the more; you have no sympathy for me in my exile. Nor have you any feeling for holy mother church, whom Our Lord God won with his own blood, enduring as she does such travail and such mortal sorrow. Nor do you pay any heed to the obedience that you say you have promised to our lord the king.[26] As long as he insists on sinning against us and against holy church, which he ought to honour, he cannot go safely into battle, he cannot exist in peace or in war without trembling for the safety of his soul.

3381 'Now I will reply to what you said in your letter about the trouble and alarm caused in the kingdom by my departure–well might they be afraid, who had worked and planned for it, lest they themselves be destroyed by it. You lavish praise on my good beginning–no sensible man is careless of his reputation, but he should rely upon himself where it is concerned, not upon others. You lay great blame on me for the wrongs I have done the king, but you do not specify them–I do not know which one to answer for. You say you are astonished that I dare to threaten our lord the king with excommunication--what father remains silent when he sees his son behaving with extreme folly? If he does not rebuke him, it is because he sees no sign of good in him. Better he should rebuke him than see him cut to bits. I am well aware that the king is willing to accept rebuke; he has no wish to suffer excommunication. God will not allow what he has planted to perish.

3399 'You see the ship beset on all sides by the gale—I am at the helm, and you ask me to go to sleep! You tell me of the kindnesses the king has done me, how he has raised me to greatness from almost nothing and has greatly advanced me—well, I will make you a child's answer to that: I was by no means so poor as you make out when our lord the king made me his high servant. I had the archdeaconry of Canterbury, the provostship of Beverley, several benefices and churches all over the kingdom, possessions and estates and other wealth—I was not at all so insignificant as you say. And if you want to talk about my poor lineage—I was born in London, of citizens of London; they lived all their lives in their neighbourhood, uncomplained of; they never grasped at other men's goods; they never injured anyone. They were not, as you assert, of the lowest possible rank. To anyone who is willing to look at things in the clear light of reason, it would seem better to come of low stock and to be good and ascend, rather than to be of high stock and to go to hell. We ought, according to the apostle, to do greater honour to our less comely members and dress them more honourably.[27] No Christian man ought to say such a thing, no man of learning, a member of a religious order, a bishop. But you reproach me perhaps with not demonstrating much intelligence—you know that it is a sin to bring shame on one's father. God said "Honour your father; your days will be the longer."[28]

3426 'There is no need for you to remind me of the kindnesses the king has done me; I can call God to witness that there is nothing in the whole world dearer to me than he is—if he will only let holy church's rights alone.

If he does not, he cannot reign in safety. No one could recount all the benefits he has done me, but even if they were multiplied a hundred times, it would not be right for me to abandon God's claims. I do not mean to spare you over this, nor anyone else, nor an angel from heaven, if one tried to sin in this matter. And if anyone asked me to do so, I would at once answer, "Satan, fly hence; your words deny God". The Lord God forbid that I should ever run so mad as to become a merchant of the body of Christ Jesus, or that my lord the king should be ruined in this way.

3441 'When I was made archbishop, raised there by God, the kingdom, you say, cried out against it, the king's mother advised against it, and holy church, as far as it lawfully might, sighed and groaned. The kingdom did not oppose it; on the contrary, it called me to the task; if the king's mother wanted to prevent it, she never said so openly, and did not appear to object; as for holy church, the only groans I heard were from those who wanted the honour themselves and failed to get it. Since then they have never stopped trying to bring me into conflict with the king. Perhaps this was their idea of revenge on me, because they had failed to satisfy their ambition. They have thwarted me ever since, and it is they who have originated and contrived all the dissension. Woe to that man by whom offences and stumbling come! They have thought up many stratagems in order to harm me, but God's strength is mightier than theirs—God, who raised me to this high station. And God, who is justice, orders and commands me not to turn my back on him for the sake of anything in the world.

3461 'I am not going to pass over your attempts to worsen my case and to justify the king. You say that he is and always has been prepared to make amends—but what kind of amends is it, always to make matters worse, and to refuse any kind of reparation? You see innocent people, widows, orphans, being exiled, blameless persons being forced to flee the country, you see many robbed of all their possessions and loaded with insults, you see my men imprisoned, bound and held fast, and clerks sent into exile—and you refuse to help them. You see your mother church being robbed and stripped of her goods and possessions, and you will not support her. You saw me, your father, whom you ought never to fail, with swords raised above my head to kill me, so that I only escaped with great difficulty, but you refused to feel any concern. But now your behaviour is worse still, your error much greater, in that you have joined with those who seek to harm me and have launched an attack upon me, against the Lord God and against his church. But you are doing it secretly, surreptitiously? You are shameless, you have cast all shame from your mind![29] Is it "amends" then to restore nothing, constantly to go from bad to worse? But you would set it down as just the opposite, perhaps, and call it "amendment" to be an eager servant to wicked men—no, this is to make one's arrows drunk with just men's blood![30]

3486 'Well may you reply, in the words of the well-tried truth, that you want to protect your coat,[31] and thus it is that you have no sword—it will not be exchanged for a sword in a hurry if you can help it. You do not imitate St. Peter, who struck at the prince's servant and cut off his ear.

3491 'You say that the king is quite ready to amend matters according to the judgment of the kingdom—I will not trust to that. No one can judge the will of God. Earthly matters can properly be tried at law, but divine things must be left to God. You ought, indeed you ought, always to warn the king that he should take care to protect the peace of holy church, that he should refrain from touching what does not concern him, and should give a great deal of thought to honouring God's priests: he should remember not who but whose they are.

3501 'You referred to the two men whom I have separated wrongly, as you say—but how rightly!—from amongst Christians. A man who sees his neighbour's cottage on fire is alarmed for his own. If I had my way, you should be moved from that ill stand that you have taken. The king must realise—and it is for you to tell him—that he who is able to rule both angels and men ordained two powers beneath him upon earth: the one is that of the priests; it must serve God; they are spiritual and men must respect them. The other is that of princes, who are of the earth only; lords, both our own and foreign, are subject to them. It is right for pagans and Christians to fear their princes. Anyone who takes from either of these orders any part of its ancient rights, undoes what the heavenly king ordained.

3516 'The king ought not to be too proud to honour those whom God in holy writ describes as gods. God calls them "god", we find it in the psalter.[32] He set up the prophet as a god against Pharaoh.[33] God demands that even speaking ill of clerks should be avoided.[34] A Jew who had sworn *per Moysen* was taken before the priests for this sin—"Take him to the gods", said the king of righteousness.[35] God's priests are described and called "god" because they are appointed and consecrated in God's place over the peoples. The king may not judge those who have the right and the power to judge him. The lips of the priest are the keepers of knowledge; the priest is the angel of God.[36] Paul, who never lies, says. "We shall judge the angels and the peoples as well"[37] God never grants to an earthly prince the keys of heaven which bind and loose: no, he delegates his might to ordained men. You would do well to make clear to the king what Constantine did, which was so praiseworthy: some priests were accused before King Constantine, the documents concerning the crime were brought to him, and the priests led into his presence—in front of everyone, he threw the writing into the blazing fire. "You are neither condemned nor judged", he said "by me. You are gods; judge your cases as it shall please yourselves. It is not right that any man should judge God". He was a good emperor! God gave him his grace, holy church exalts him, and he sees God face to face. The king ought to imitate his way of life and example. Otherwise he must tremble at God's threat: whoever shall presumptuously refuse to listen to his priest and his judge, shall die.[38] God establishes the king over the kingdom so that he shall maintain the peace which God sends us. This is the only way for the king to win salvation, however great his strength or mighty his power, or even if all the kingdoms that exist were under his governance.

3554 'And the answer that I have made to you in this letter, I make also to all those who have taken your side. Now I beg and pray you, my brothers, equally,[39] that there may be no jealousy, dissension or deceit amongst us, but that within us there may be, in God, one heart and one soul. Let us listen to God, who asks us to die for justice. He has begun the battle against our enemies for our sakes. My brothers, do not let us forget this true Judge. When sinners and righteous shall appear before him at the end of this world, on the last day, he will judge the world. He will not then stand in awe of any king, any prince, or mighty emperor.'

Garnier Reflects on Custom

3566 Such were the letters that the prelates who ought to protect holy church sent to the saint across the sea. They aimed at setting up the customs of the realm in holy mother church. But the most holy baron fought constantly to prevent this and to set her free. Custom, clearly, is not law, for any powerful man who refuses to fear God imposes any custom that he likes upon his people—here I see one custom, there another. But God does not love custom, he loves a firm basis of truth. And how short is the life of poor miserable man—he is now hot, now cold, like lukewarm water—and so it is a very great sin to set up a custom which causes any man harm or injures anyone, for it may be breaking his heart, but he cannot remove it. If King Henry wants to retain his ancestors' customs, I would like to know which he means to set up in his kingdom—those of the Red King, the fool, or those of Henry the Old King, the mighty.[40] The Red King left the churches nothing at all; he took their rents, their possessions, their gold and silver, and made the clerks pay ransom. God avenged it all—he was killed by an arrow and ended evilly, his body is rotten and his soul in agony. And if it is his customs that King Henry has adopted, and he wants to make war on the clergy and holy church, vengeance will strike him before he knows what is happening. God has already set his arrow to the bow—he slays both body and soul, his justice is swift and fierce. King Henry the Old took other men's wives and forbade their lawful husbands to come near them; he killed men for the sake of dumb beasts; he sinned many and many a time against holy church. If his grandson copies him, between him and God be it! We cannot deny that Henry the Old had a priest hanged who was exceedingly wicked, and in order too to frighten such as would not leave off their wrongdoing. But although a custom may be fixed because of some wrong act, yet bad customs and bad usages are certainly to be avoided.

3604 Well, now let us stop discussing customs, and the three prelates whom you heard me name; I do not mean to talk about their behaviour any more. I want to tell you about the holy Archbishop, who remained in exile beyond the sea for six years.

CHAPTER SIX

Pontigny and Sens

3611 THE HOLY MAN stayed at Pontigny for two years,[1] but he kept his way of life secret from everyone, clerk or lay, and even from his own associates as far as he could. He fled from and avoided all bodily comfort and afflicted himself night and day in God's service. He now began seriously to ill-treat his body, and to eat only coarse foods such as cabbages and turnips. He used to have good dishes removed secretly and taken to the poor folk in the town—secretly, because his clerks would have reproached him if they had known about it. They did often remonstrate with him over the life he was leading, because he was extremely weak and was much too severe with himself. He was cutting off, they said, his own men's heads; they had been driven out for his sake and if he were to die on them now, not one of them would ever be able to get back to his own country. There was a stream there, running from one building to another,[2] and he used to bathe in it in the evening to chill his flesh; one evening he had William of Capes in attendance on him, and he said,

'My lord, you want to cut our very hearts!' After that, he never took him with him again, because of his rebuke. But then one of his cheeks became all festered, so much so that the inside of his mouth was putrid right to the teeth; it made him very ill for a long time. William pulled out two small bones, and he got better. I have heard this spoken of, in order that it might be known.

3636 One night, when he was weary with prayer and had fallen asleep, he had a vision—he and the king, who hated him without reason, were standing before the Pope engaged in an angry dispute; all the cardinals were opposing him wildly—he thought they were trying to dig his eyes out of his head with their fingers. Only the Pope, who thoroughly understood his case, stood up for him, but he could not hear his voice; their uproar and shouting had made him hoarse. Next he was alone in the consistory, no living man with him; then evil murderers were sent to him and he thought they cut off his tonsure with their swords. Truly he had God's promise that he should be killed in his quarrel and for holy church.

3651 One of the lay brothers of the monastery—they did not tell me his name—had been very much troubled with a serious illness, and his abdomen was all swollen by the dropsy. Winter and summer he prayed to the mother of God, asking her to pray to her son to give him health. Night and day he besought the mother of the Creator to send him health in his pain, till one night the lady of sweetness visited him; she told him to go at once to Thomas and to get him to touch him all over the abdomen with his hands. Next day the brother went to the holy man, and found him in his study; there he begged and prayed him, for the pity of God, until the baron did put his hand on the man's abdomen; the brother held and guided it. He gave him something to drink—I do not know for certain what it was—and almost at once the brother fell down; he vomited an astonishing quantity of poison and filth and then lay still for a long time. Then he stood up, thin, cured of his illness by the holy man's hands. He cured many sick people with the food left from his meals; a rich man's daughter who had had a fever for many a long week was completely cured by this means. There was not a man in the country suffering from debilitating fever, however bad it might be, who could not obtain certain health from the remains of his meals.

Thomas Forced to Leave Pontigny

3676 But when King Henry realised that Thomas would be able to stay indefinitely at Pontigny—neither he nor his dependents lacked anything, and King Louis and the French had come to his aid—he resolved to pluck him out of that nest as soon as he could.[3] There is, I have heard, a very ancient custom whereby all white abbots gather at Cîteaux every third year from both sides of the sea, the reason being that all the rest must submit to this one and guide their order in everything according to his advice.[4] In the second year of the baron's exile, when he had been nearly two years at Pontigny, the king, who hated him bitterly, had by no means forgotten about him; he wrote to that abbot of whom I told you, informing him that he was maintaining his mortal enemy, let him take good note of this; and he assured him emphatically that if he were to maintain his enemy any longer, or allow him to find a refuge anywhere in their order, he would send to him every white monk and every abbot in his land, not one of them should remain. When the letter was read out and made known in their hearing, the abbots all fell at the feet of the great abbot and each one begged for mercy, for himself and for them all; they besought him not to allow them all to be ruined, nor to let them lose all the work they had done, because of one man. They discussed the matter together and came to a decision: they would not expose themselves to so great a loss—the loss of their possessions, their daughter houses, their country, the destruction of the places they had won for God; it would be better that one man rather than so many should be made miserable. They would provide for all that he and his people might need in some other place a long way away from themselves. (I am sure that the king had had them all told that he would expel them from his land if they did not send the Archbishop away.) Garin the abbot[5] listened to this decision to turn the Archbishop out of Pontigny, and he addressed the abbot of Cîteaux proudly:

3714 'It cannot be', he said, 'we cannot order that the friend of God he turned away for this cause. Pope Alexander commended him to us and he has been with us now for nearly two years. We have seen no sign that we have suffered in any way because of him or his people, neither as regards wine or corn. We have never had less spoilt in a comparable period of time. It was for the sake of Christianity, which he was endeavouring to uphold, that King Henry made him flee from his country. Our order was established for the sole purpose of helping and supporting those in need, and we ought not to fail this man for any reason whatever.' But in spite of Sir Garin the abbot they did not refrain from carrying out the decision made in common council. (Guichard, the previous abbot, was now archbishop of the city of Lyons, for Saint Thomas had recommended him to the Pope.) The abbot of Cîteaux sent word to Saint Thomas by Sir Garin the abbot, telling him everything that was in the letter, how the king threatened to ruin them all; now he begged him for God's sake to advise him what course would be best for them all, both on the one side and on the other. The Archbishop had been told all about it already, for his messengers had been present at the chapter and had listened to the proceedings.

3739 'It would be a very great sin', he said to the abbot, 'if so many good men were ruined just for my sake. May Jesus Christ the merciful be grateful to you for the kindnesses you and yours have done to me and to mine; we have lacked nothing, neither food nor clothing. God will guide me, he is always near me; he brings down the proud and raises the poor man from the dungheap.'

3746 'Do not distress yourself, my lord', said the abbot. 'This order may mean that you must be sent away, but it shall be to some place where you and all your people shall be supplied liberally, better than you were before.'

'May the divine pity', he said, 'be grateful to you.'

Louis Welcomes Thomas to France

3751 The king of France was told how the king had had him sent away from Pontigny, and when he heard about it, the king thanked God: now he would be able to do as he wished and give the Archbishop what he had more than once offered him. For when Thomas had first fled from England the king of France had often asked him, both personally and through others, clerks and friends, to stay with him in St. Denis's kingdom; he would never have to beg for anything he needed. But he had at that time refused the king's offers, for he very much feared that Henry the proud king would allege that he had gone to King Louis and made alliance with him, solely in order to wage war on him. But now he would not hesitate to accept his offer. When the king of France heard that he was being driven out and he would be able to have him, he clasped his hands together and raised them in thanksgiving to God who rules the world.

3769 'I can believe', he said, 'that the angels may lose their faith!' He said this because of the way the monks had behaved. Then King Louis mounted his horse, took his men with him, and went to Pontigny.[6] He went into the chapter meeting with the holy Archbishop, and earnestly thanked the abbot and all the monks for the honour with which they had treated the baron. They had, he said, done France a very great honour, by making this good lord welcome amongst them. He did not want them to find in future that they had brought upon themselves the enmity of King Henry, who was trying to ruin them because they loved him; he hoped that from now on he would make his home with him. He would take him with him to Sens, he said, and would see that he was provided with all that he needed, both he and his people, whatever they might require. Hearing that he was to go, almost all the lords wept with sorrow.

3786 Then the king sent his men to Sens, to Ste. Colombe,[7] and had accommodation prepared where the holy man could stay. Servants and butlers were sent for to supply him from Louis's resources with whatever he needed. When King Louis was quite sure that he would have the Archbishop's company, he went back into France, and the Archbishop got ready for his journey. He went with his household to Ste. Colombe and was treated with great respect all the time he stayed with them. The abbey of Ste. Colombe is near Sens; it is a foundation of black monks. Four years did he stay there,[8] the baron who trusted only in Christ, and his way of life was in no way worsened. The abbot and the monks found it very pleasant to have him with them.

Henry and Louis

3801 When King Henry saw that Thomas would be able to remain with King Louis, who found everything he and his people needed out of his own private wealth, he was sad at heart, I can tell you. He should not stay there long if he could help it! He exerted all his strength, and sent his son Henry to the king in France, to become the king's son's man, as his baron, holding the lands across the sea of him.[9] What jewels you would have seen being exchanged between them, and hounds sent from one to the other, and hawks taken to and fro! And King Henry gave so much to the French barons that by dint of lavish generosity he made them all his friends, and thought he had got hold of the whole council of the country. After that the kings arranged to hold a meeting, which took place at St.-Léger-en-Yvelines.[10] There they bound themselves to be firm friends for ever, and they both swore that neither of them would ever in future keep in his kingdom any enemy of the other. After this they went away. They planned a further meeting, at Tours,[11] but this time the French did not attend—King Louis had been advised not to do so, as he had no castle or stronghold in the district; they did not know what the king of England had in mind. Then King Henry summoned him to keep the agreement, saying that he had not kept what he had sworn to, in that he had welcomed his mortal enemy, a man who was a rebel, a traitor to the whole realm. The king said that this question had never been raised, nor had the Archbishop been mentioned at the conference; he had carefully observed all items of the agreement; but if any man were convicted of treason and sentenced to leave his country, he should not receive support in any part of their lands.

3836 When the Archbishop heard that King Henry was trying to have him expelled from France, and going to such trouble about it, he had a letter written to him. He told him that his efforts were in vain, he would never deprive him of his bread; God, who would never fail him, would always give him sufficient. He had been much comforted by a man who went to see him and told him that he would provide for all his needs, and the needs of 20 more men than he had, and would moreover give five hundred pounds of pennies with which to provide for the rest of his personal necessities. And another man promised him just as much; he would never fail him for any man at any time. He did not fear the English or the French king, nor any German, north or south, duke or emperor. But the good king of France provided for him in his retreat.

A Vision and a Nightmare

3851 One day when he had striven hard in prayer and lay grieving, as his custom was, before the altar in deep devotion, he received a true revelation of God. He showed himself to him and called him twice by his own name, 'Thomas'.

'You will raise up my church', he said to him, 'in your blood'.

'Who are you, lord, who have come to me here?'

'I am Jesus, your brother. You will glorify my church by your blood, and you will be exalted.'

'May it be so!' said Thomas.

3861 On another occasion he dreamed a dream at Ste. Colombe (the man to whom he told it repeated it faithfully to me): he thought he stood in the consistory, pleading at law, and his opponent was the king of England. The king attacked him cruelly as the case went on, and Hilary of Chichester attacked him bitterly, and so did Gilbert Foliot of London. All the cardinals took the king's side—in the whole court he had no friend but Pope Alexander, the only one who supported him. But he shouted at them so much, and they at him, that he became quite hoarse with the noise and the shouting. Hilary of Chichester became dumb during the hearing; as for the bishop of London, all his flesh went rotten, and his whole body disintegrated and fell into little pieces. And then the king at once had Saint Thomas seized and had his head skinned all round with knives. But the baron was not hurt, he felt no pain, and he laughed, which made the king furious. Then the saint woke up, terrified. And we have indeed seen the Pope weakening in this cause, because he could not support the Archbishop against them all; we have seen Hilary of Chichester become dumb and repent of the harm he had done the martyr.[12] Now let London take care, lest his flesh fall off! But I think I understand this falling correctly: he has come to repent little by little, and this is the piecemeal diminution of his flesh. But let him take care to make full amends, otherwise God will exact lawful vengeance.

Thomas's Sufferings

3891 The holy man remained in a foreign land for six years. He endured a very harsh life, which he was careful to conceal even from those in his confidence. There were very few men, laymen or lettered—indeed, only three men[13]—to whom he revealed the truth of his existence. The holy man never had his servants woken in the morning when he got up, or when he put on his clothes and his shoes. He would go into the church, to his first task, and there he reverently did the work of the Lord God; he would never neglect this for any reason. About noon each day he sang his mass, and was in all things earnestly bent on serving his Lord. He used to spend the best part of the day in his oratory, in a small room, where he did his work; he would shut the door, but he was not resting. When he was in there, he would lay himself down in prayer, in tears and weeping and in grief. No one but God knew the nature of the distress he caused his body and how he suffered. The baron was wholly given up to contemplation. He used to come out of this room at mealtimes, not in order to fill or fatten his body, but because he wanted to encourage his household, and to see the hungry poor and help them. His own way of living he kept quite hidden. He used to drink the best wine he could get, but this was so as to warm his cold stomach (for his stomach and body were always exceedingly cold; he used to eat ginger and clove by handfuls). None the less, he always drank his wine *[3920]* watered. Then when the holy man had risen from the table he never wanted to listen to any song or story, or anything else that was not true. He preferred to hear tell of the spiritual king and to look upon those writings which endure for ever. Then when day was plunged into night and Saint Thomas's bed was made ready on a leather-covered bedstead, with an embroidered quilt, a thin layer of straw, and expensive linen sheets, white and finely woven, then Archbishop Thomas gave himself up to prayer and deep grief until he was worn out, and he would lie down to sleep on the bare ground in the same clothes that he had worn all day; he did not change them. No one, high or low, realised how he lived. He wore sharp prickly drawers made out of coarse goats' hair, and another hair garment as well which covered his whole body, back and front, and his arms, too, down past his elbows. It was full of knots and clusters of vermin, which prevented his flesh from ever getting any repose. *[3940]* And he forced his body to suffer more than this: every night he disciplined his flesh, whipping and tearing it with sharp thongs. Robert of Merton[14] could tell the truth about this; he did not dare trespass against holy obedience. Robert of Merton was his chaplain and was in his closest confidence; he slept in his room. But when he came to die, when he beheld the great agony, then for the first time he revealed it, for he had promised him never to disclose his way of living during his lifetime. After Robert had gone to bed, the baron would cause himself endless pain, he said, when he ought to have been resting; a good third of the night he would go on without stopping. Then he would come across to Robert and get him up and hand him the scourge with which to discipline him. He would beat him till he was exhausted, deeply moved with compassion, sweating with distress; then he would throw down the thongs with their knotted ends.

3960 'Wretch', Thomas would say then, 'why was I ever born? Of all the wretches in the world, I am the most miserable!' But even when the chaplain had gone to bed, Saint Thomas still would give himself no respite—he would begin to hack bits off his body himself, tearing his flesh with his hands. Little did he care about his flesh, when his heart was so loyal! And when this Robert was about to make his confession he revealed that the saint had never had peace for a single day or night since he had received the burden of consecration, but had always been beaten four or five times, or three at the very least; he refused all remission. Such was the life led by Our Lord's vassal. He had a bath, however, every fortieth day, and changed his hair clothes, because of the vermin and the sweat; he used to put on fresh ones which he kept in reserve. He suffered constant pain and distress for God's sake. Such was this holy man's life and suffering. He never revealed it or spoke of it to any man under heaven, except, as I have heard tell, to his servant, Brun, who washed his hair clothes and served him in that way, and to Robert his priest, who flogged him at night.

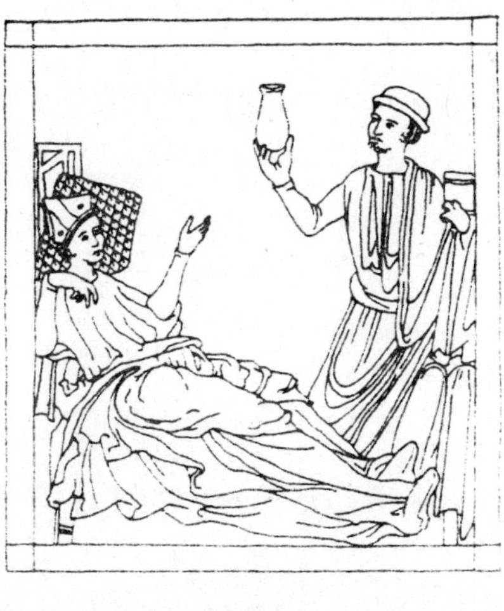

CHAPTER SEVEN

Attempts at Reconciliation

3981 BUT IN THE MEANTIME Louis, the greatly respected king of France, was doing all he could to restore friendship between the king and Saint Thomas. The Pope had sent several letters to the meetings they had held concerning the agreement between them. A conference was to meet at Pontoise;[1] the Pope travelled as far as Paris to go to it. The Archbishop, on whose account it was arranged, was there. But when King Henry heard that the Pope was to be present, he went away again. He then arranged a meeting between himself and King Louis at Nogent-le-Rotrou,[2] to deal with business of his own. St. Denis's king took the Archbishop to this meeting, so as to reconcile him and the king, if he could. But the king of England was not interested in reconciliation, and requested the king of France to stop raising this matter of Thomas the Archbishop, as he did not wish to discuss it; he would then do anything for him that he might ask.

4000 'I shall be glad to stop', answered Louis the baron. 'Neither he nor his people are any trouble to me and I shall be very happy to be able to keep him. My kingdom benefits from his great wisdom, and yours is all the poorer for its loss–I daresay you will find your need greater than mine.'

The noble king of France went to see the Archbishop and said to him,

4007 'I shall never count any more upon your being reconciled, although I had always hoped for it until now; but I have found the king of England altogether above himself. He refuses to listen to me, either privately or in public audience. I have often begged you to stay in St. Denis's kingdom—now I make over my kingdom and my country to you absolutely, Etampes and Orléans, Chartres and Paris. Your needs shall be supplied from my rents and my resources.'

4016 After this a meeting was held at Montmirail.[3] Two cardinals joined the king there from Rome: William of Pavia and Sir John of Naples.[4] They both supported King Henry wholeheartedly and would have been delighted to deceive the Archbishop. The king told them that he intended to humble himself: he would agree to do for the Archbishop anything that they should decide and that holy church should wish, always supposing that the Archbishop would accept this.

'He will', they said, 'he cannot do anything else.'

4026 On the night before the day fixed for this meeting, Saint Thomas stayed at Chartres,[5] with the retinue he had brought with him. There God showed him a vision by which he knew for certain, as he told his confidential companions, what the result of next day's talks would be. It seemed to him that he and the king were standing together somewhere, and the king held out to him a very handsome golden or gilded cup full of wine and asked him to drink. He looked at the wine and saw that it was so muddy that he did not dare drink it, and refused to take it. Then, after examining the cup all round, and being alarmed at the muddiness of the wine, he saw two identical spiders crawl up out of it; one of them sat on one rim, one on the other.

4040 'Take it away', he said, 'I don't want to drink that filth.' In the morning he sent for his friends and his clerks and told them the dream he had had in the night. 'I know', he said, 'just how this meeting will go. The king will make us wonderful offers, but I shall not accept them, because it is all a trick. The beautiful gilt cup that he tried to give me stands for the fine offers I shall refuse, the muddy wine is the treachery he is preparing. And those two huge spiders are the two wicked cardinals, who mean to deceive us if they can.'

4051 When he arrived at the conference, he found the cardinals present. King Henry[6] said that he would be happy to refer the matter to these two, and to abide by whatever decisions they might come to, and whatever holy church should decide. He perceived the deception clearly, and guarded against it. The cardinals were trying to force him into a trap; they said that he could not refuse their decision, or refuse to accept what holy church would decide. He said that he had no wish to oppose holy church, or to obtain anything but what was reasonable from the king; but, he said, he preferred not to enter into any plea until such time as the king should fully restore, return and give back to him and to his people all that was theirs, in the same condition that they had left it in at the time that he had had them expelled from England. He would on no account plead as a dispossessed man. The king would not hear of agreeing to this, but wanted him to accept the two cardinals' decision. He, however, refused to abide by their pronouncement. And so he went away; he could do nothing more.

4071 Another meeting was held at Montmirail,[7] arranged by the Pope, who wrote letters about it. King Louis was present, with the French barons; and King Henry, with many great magnates. Many great clerks and famous barons were there, for the Pope had sent from Rome Sir Bernard de la Coudre,[8] a good and holy man; the prior of the Mont-Dieu,[9] a most honourable person; and archbishops, bishops, priors and abbots, in order to make this peace. They worked hard in the attempt. What Saint Thomas was asking for were the rights of holy church, her possessions and estates that the king had taken; what the king wanted was that the customs should be established in the kingdom—he would not relinquish one jot of his customs. Saint Thomas said that he did not intend to commit so great a wrong. Clerks and laymen went to and fro between them all day, till at last the king said that all he cared about was the honour involved: let

Thomas simply do for him what his predecessors had done for his. It was necessary for him that his people *[4090]* should fear him, therefore he had to appear to be cruel and harsh; he had an exceedingly troublesome people to rule, and for that reason had to put on a show of great severity. But if the Archbishop would consent to grant to him the same that his predecessors, Lanfranc and the holy Anselm,[10] had observed for his ancestors, he would not ask anything more. The Archbishop replied: please God he would never be bound to observe something of which he was ignorant; it was right to imitate them in what they had done that was good, but he did not mean to copy their mistakes; in this world every man at some time must err. St. Peter the apostle, whom God honoured with the gift of power both in heaven and earth, denied Jesus Christ his lord three times. He would not do that for anything in the world; nor would he ever keep customs contrary to reason. He could not, he said, specify a single one of these customs which his predecessors had had to keep for the kings. The king said that he would have them sworn to by 200 men, knights and priests. He might, the baron replied, find plenty of men to swear, but he was not going to refer holy church to their oath.

4112 'My lords', the king said at this, 'he does not want peace. Look what affection and generosity I am showing him!' And then they all cried out together against the Archbishop, both clerks and laymen shouting at him that he was too aggressive. When the Archbishop saw that they had all turned against him and not one of them would stand by him, he gave a heartfelt sigh, and wept; and prayed to Jesus Christ, whom holy church adores, that his words might not lead him into sin against God. King Henry then said that he would refer himself to the decision of any three French bishops[11] he should select; he would agree to whatever they should decide on. They all cried out then, saying he had done enough. Saint Thomas said that France possessed many excellent men, and he would indeed agree to their decision; he would keep the customs, saving his order. The king swore that this expression must be dropped; it was an equivocation, he said, with which he meant to cheat him. Everyone *[4130]* called out to him from every side that he should leave that phrase out. Then the holy Archbishop conceded to him that he would observe the customs, saving his fidelity to God—the king swore by the eyes that this phrase should not be allowed, 'for there is sophistry in it', he said, 'and great duplicity', But how can there ever be duplicity in faithfulness to God? After this the Archbishop said that he would do for him all that any Archbishop ought to do for his king—the king swore by the eyes that this expression must go, for it covered treachery, he said, and guile. But a man who does 'all that he ought' is plotting no guile! The king said that all he asked was that he should do him honour; just let him do for him what his predecessors had done for the kings, what the best of them had done for the very worst. And all the wisest and best men spoke out and said that the king had done enough; he wanted to reach a settlement and was offering friendship. When the Archbishop saw that every one of them sided with the king, the prior of the Mont-Dieu and Bernard de la Coudre and even the king of France, upon whom he had relied more than on anyone, tears fell from his fine eyes, and he collected his thoughts in silence.

4150 'My lords', he said to them, 'I agree to his wish.'

After the Archbishop had surrendered to the king like this, and agreement had been reached on both sides, the Archbishop bared his head, and King Henry did the same; then they approached each other in order to exchange the kiss of peace and true friendship. The Archbishop, ever close to God, said,

'My lord, I kiss you to the honour of God and of yourself.'

Geoffrey Ridel[12] said, 'There's sophistry in that!'

4159 'God's eyes! It's true, he does not want peace', and the king wheeled his horse round and spurred away. Both clerks and laymen, seeing the king of England go off like that, blamed the Archbishop severely, saying that he had done wrong in not abiding by his agreement, and that no one could blame King Henry; they had never known an agreement abandoned for such a trifle. Saint Thomas lost all the French that day; they called him traitor and double-dealer all over France. Our Lord's vassal returned to his lodging. His clerks were unhappy and angry with him; they told him that he had killed them all without hope of reprieve.

4171 'You are quite wrong', he said; 'I think you must all be blind. The Lord God has preserved us from great shame today; hitherto the king has constantly attacked us, and called us traitors and wicked men; now he has freed us from this and set it aside. He now asks nothing from us but that we should do him honour, that we should keep the customs as our predecessors did; and we agreed to this. But it will never come to this, never. Thanks be to the Creator that we have escaped such disgrace!'

4181 Then he had a letter written sending word to the Pope, and telling him all that he had granted to the king for the sake of peace, and the reason why the king had drawn back and refused it and had expressly excluded God from his peace. Now he asked him to let him know what he wanted him to do.

The king stayed the night at La Ferté-Bernard. He drew Geoffrey Ridel forward and said to his companions,

4188 'I want you all to honour this man. He has shown himself today to be worth more than gold tried seven times in the fire: his good sense saved me, and the traitor did not manage to deceive me.'

4191 When he had gone to bed, and had thought over all that the Archbishop had conceded to him, and how he had rejected it because of one single expression, he exclaimed suddenly that he had been mistaken and had acted wrongly, because the Archbishop had done what he wanted; and he swore by God's eyes and said he was certain he would never be able to get back to that situation. He woke all his servants at once and sent for the bishop of Poitiers;[13] he was to come and see him quickly. He came immediately, at midnight.

4202 'You must go to the Archbishop', King Henry said. 'I made a mistake in not granting him peace, for he gave me all I could possibly ask him. God's eyes! I shall never get that again. Go after him now, put your mind to it; tell him I will now accept what he offered me yesterday.' The bishop mounted at once, and sent word ahead that he was coming. When Saint Thomas heard this, he had his pack mules loaded and set off without waiting for him. The bishop followed him hot foot; when he caught up with him, Thomas answered that no one could induce him to return to the situation in which they had had him, for it was contrary to reason.

4216 On another occasion King Henry went to pray at St.-Denis-en-France,[14] and King Louis went to St. Denis to see him. He begged him, for the sake of the saints to whom he had been praying, to allow himself and the Archbishop to be made friends. After this the two kings met at Montmartre,[15] where they completed the discussion of some business left unfinished[16] at St.-Léger-en-Yvelines. When this was done, the king of France spoke to him in a friendly way about Thomas the Archbishop, expressing the wish that they be reconciled. The king of England said,

4226 'If all the wrongs he has done to me and to the men of my fief were put right, we could then very well reach an agreement, if you advise it.' The good king of France said,

4229 'If everything on both sides were to be brought up again, there would never be amity. It is very shocking that there should be this bitter enmity between you: why cannot everything on both sides be forgiven, and neither of you make any demands?' The king of England said,

4234 'I will refer myself to the decision of the clergy.' And so clerks were sent for from Paris.[17] They arrived, and the king was informed; but the king of England would not say a word to them. The good king of France, however, would not let him remain silent; he told him that he was acting most wrongly towards God, in showing no affection or loyalty to his Archbishop; and he kept on at him until at last the king of England agreed to give back to Thomas and to his people one half of all the income that he had taken from him, and to refer himself to the court of Rome for the other half. He promised faithfully that he would see that he and his people should receive this property without fail; it should be entirely available for their needs and at their disposal; they should have peace and love from himself and from his heir.

4250 'I will tell him this', said King Louis. And then the king reported all this to the Archbishop, and it was agreed on both sides that it should be so. Then the king of France said,

'If you want friendship, all that is now lacking is that you should kiss each other.' King Henry said,

'I am not going to agree to that. I have vowed', he said, 'never to kiss him. I will get my son to give him a hundred kisses on my behalf; I will keep peace and love towards him and his; I will give them back their property and their incomes; this does not mean that I shall ever hold them the less dear.'

4261 The good king went to tell the Archbishop about this, and Saint Thomas answered that the kiss did not matter, as long as he would grant him peace and love, and as long as future events should show him to be sincere.

4266 (The meeting arranged for this settlement took place close by Fréteval, near the Beauce area.[18] Louis, the good king, was there with the French contingent, and King Henry with his barons; the best of the clergy of both countries were present.)

4271 But in the evening, back at their lodgings, his clerks blamed him very much and reproached him for not making peace with the king, and for having no pity on them. Master Gunther[19] was one of those who took him up about this, and the holy Archbishop answered him as follows:

4276 'You are longing to be in England, Master Gunther', he said, 'and I can quite understand it; but believe me, you would not have been there 40 days before you would give 500 marks of silver to be out of it again.'

4281 The Archbishop then sent word to the Pope,[20] telling him how he had behaved towards the king and how it had turned out; then he asked him to send to the king, in his holy kindness, and tell him that his sins should all be forgiven and that he should give the Archbishop the kiss of peace and security. Wise man that the baron was, he asked the Pope to command him upon holy obedience to enter the king's presence and to give the kiss of peace. He gave this letter to Madoc,[21] who hastened to make the journey and presented it to the Pope as soon as he had permission to do so. The Pope at once had his own letter written:[22] he told King Henry, lord of England, to kiss Thomas, Archbishop of Canterbury, in peace, and to forgive him without reservations all anger and all ill feeling; might Jesus Christ heal him of all his sins; let him return to Thomas, and to his people as well, all their property, everything they might specify, leaving nothing out; he had both reason and power to lay his land under an interdict—and not one land only, but his whole empire; he could never refuse justice, for the sake of any man. He sent word to Saint Thomas: upon holy obedience, if he could obtain peace, he must not refuse it; he must make every effort and not allow himself to despair. For the Pope was very tired of this warfare; he was not getting the value of a single penny out of England.

4306 Next the Pope sent William, archbishop of Sens,[23] a man of true nobility, without equal for goodness and honour in all France, together with the bishop of Nevers[24] and several others whose names I do not know, to King Henry in order to arrange the settlement. King Henry gave them his word that he would gladly do what they advised and what the Pope ordered. Eventually, after much discussion, they decided to hold a further meeting not far from the Beauce region.[25] Archbishop Thomas attended it with his company, as did King Louis with many great barons, and the king of England with his mighty men, and archbishops, bishops, and learned clerks, all in order to settle the peace, if God had so ordained it. King Louis and the archbishops, bishops and other clergy all harassed King Henry to such an extent that he said he would now do all that they recommended. (He was afraid of the Pope, who had threatened him.)

4325 'Nothing is lacking', they said, 'except that you have not kissed him.' The king said that he would not kiss him for the sake of any man on earth; he could not and ought not to do so; he had vowed he would not—and so he refused the request of King Louis, his lord. But before he went away he would do him such honour instead of the kiss as should be worth a hundred kisses. They worked so hard on both sides to reach an agreement—Louis, the good king, and the bishops and abbots—that the king and Saint Thomas did actually meet. As soon as they saw each other, they came forward and met, and King Henry greeted him, and he greeted the king. When everyone on both sides, clerk and knight, thought that the king was going to give Thomas the kiss of true peace, he said,

4338 'My lord Archbishop, I would like a word with you', and led him into the middle of the field, out of all the dust. They did not call for anyone, and nobody liked to go near them. The king and Saint Thomas stopped there so long talking of one thing and another, their voices rising and falling, that both parties became very tired of waiting for them. They even got down twice off their plump palfreys, and then remounted again, so that all those watching said, 'This is absurd!' When the Archbishop remounted, the king held his stirrup for him, and as Thomas was trying to stop him, the king said:

'No, I insist; you are my father in God, I must do you honour.' Everyone who saw this thought it was a very good sign.

4351 Saint Thomas, sitting there on horseback talking with the king, kept shifting his seat from one side to the other, with one thigh on the saddle and the other hanging down; the reason was that his hair drawers were hurting him very much, but those who did not know this thought it showed great disrespect.

4356 Saint Thomas and the king remained a long time in close conversation alone in the middle of the field; they did not send for a single one of all their people. I do not know all the details of what they said, but will tell you a part of the truth, as far as I know it. When the king had taken him out alone into the middle of the field, he said,

4362 'My lord Archbishop, your absence has been much felt. Other counsels have caused me great harm; nothing has gone right with me since I lost yours. I have been involved in great expense and waste.' The true priest spoke out courageously:

4367 'My lord king', he said to him, 'you shall forsake all such counsels, and in future you shall have different counsellors, such as will always speak out against your wishes, whose advice shall never contain one word of what you desire.'

4371 'From now on', said the king, 'I shall pay no attention to any advice but yours, and will trust to it alone. Indeed, I would wish to give you my whole realm in charge; I want to entrust my son Henry and the care of him to you—I have not got a foot of land left, I must go and provide for myself.'

4376 'Indeed!' said Saint Thomas, 'that's very likely—you would leave your kingdom, which is so dear to you, and your young children who need you so much, and go into other lands to challenge other men's rights? This is certainly not a course I would advise you to take.'

'God's eyes!' he said, 'I will relinquish it all, and make my son and my kingdom over to you.'

4383 'I promise you', said Saint Thomas, 'I will never accept it. I will never have anything more to do with earthly honours, for I am already overburdened with the task I have. But if you do want to leave your land and your kingdom to go and serve God, if you want to take the cross, I advise you to put your kingdom and your son into the care of Hugh de Beauchamp,[26] who is a

loyal knight, and I will help them to guide the kingdom.'
4391 The two of them argued about many things, of which I have not yet been exactly informed; and my book cannot anyhow contain everything. The king accused him on many grounds; and he made bitter complaints against the king–concerning his clerks and himself, who had been exiled and had not got so much as six inches of their estates; concerning his men, who had been ill-treated, arrested, bound; and even little children who had been driven out along with their mothers and fathers–he had no mercy on them.
4401 'It is all owing to your own misconduct', King Henry said to him. 'You absconded from my kingdom, when no one had done you any harm. That was why I sent your relatives and friends to you. But it will all be put right when you come back.'

'My lord', said the Archbishop, 'what about your son? You had him anointed and crowned king in great haste and quite uselessly, so as to injure me.'

'That was wrong', said the king, 'I can see that now. But if it is my duty to make amends, then this can perfectly well be done.'
4411 'What have you to say', he asked, 'about the three men who crowned him in order to please you, and to take away from the holy mother church of Holy Trinity her rights and her age-old dignity of the anointing of kings?' King Henry answered him,

'I shall never interfere any more as regards you or the bishops; from now on I shall keep my mouth shut on this score. Exercise your rights; I leave it all to yourself.'

Both parties were saying that the two had reached an agreement, for the king's manner towards him appeared thoroughly friendly.
4421 After he had talked with the Archbishop long enough, the king arranged that they should meet again at Tours;[27] there, he said, everything should be completed and all wrongs put right; there the archbishop should receive such letters as he wished. They came away from that place in peace and amity, the king holding his

stirrup for him when he mounted. Then people in both parties begged the king to kiss the Archbishop, but he said he would not, he did not wish to kiss him at that time, he had sworn not to do to. When he went to Tours, then he would kiss him.

4431 After this the bishop of Lisieux went up to Thomas and said to him,

'My lord Archbishop, please would you listen to me? God through his grace has reconciled the king and yourself; now here is Geoffrey Ridel, who has been at variance with you—we ask you to forgive him.'

'My lord bishop', he said, 'I know him to be suspended. If he wishes to make amends for his error, I will accept that, and will thereafter do all that I ought for him.'

'Never mind', said Geoffrey, 'if he hates me, I'll hate him—if he wants to be my friend, I will be his.'

4441 The night before the meeting was due to take place, three leagues from Tours, as it had been arranged, Thomas stayed at Tours with his trusted companions. He went this way because of Rotrou the archbishop, and it proved a very thorough test of the king's intentions. For the king was behaving to him with every appearance of good will, so that everyone, high and low, said that the king would never hate him any more all his life long—and so Saint Thomas went to Tours on the previous night, to find out whether he meant what he said. That was why he went and stayed that night at Tours; and also to find out whether or not the king would there grant him the kiss. But he brought neither pence nor halfpence with him. He had now either to pay or to abandon his debts. The king did not kiss him; and he did not pay what he owed.[28] This made Our Lord's vassal extremely anxious, and he had his pack animals loaded at daybreak, ordering them to be taken straight back again. The king was standing looking out of this high palace and he saw his pastor's men travelling so early, and Thomas himself following fast behind them. He sent a messenger after him quickly, telling him to wait, because he wanted to talk to him. But he went on a league before he would stop, and turned off the road to sing his hours. They waited for the king in an open green space, and sang their hours, without dismounting. The king went straight to him as soon as he saw him; king and archbishop went forward to meet each other, and exchanged greetings.

4471 'In the name of the Three Persons', said the king, 'there are three of us here.' For Saint Thomas had the prelate of Rouen there with him—he was called Rotrou, I believe—so that there were three of them, those two, and the king. Their clerks kept back in a group.

4476 'King', said Saint Thomas, 'you are ill advised. You are not the same man that you used to be in the days when I worked for you; you are very much altered—I have left my debts in your city. Louis would not have done it, not if he had had to pawn his fiefs.' The king smiled (whether sincerely or not I do not know) and said,

4482 'My lord Archbishop, how angry you are! But be patient, everything shall be put right. I have been so much preoccupied with other business that I could not attend to you, not for fiefs or lands.' When they had talked together as long as they wished, they all remounted and set off; the king went back and they continued their journey.

4489 They met next day, however, at Amboise[29] and there, as far as appearances and words go, they were reconciled. All the conditions were set down there, and the king agreed to them all fully, in the hearing of everyone present; he granted a letter about this, with his seal appended, which was sent to his justices and to his son. Richard Malban[30] and Hugh the clerk took it.[31] If you would like to hear this letter, I can tell it you exactly, just as the king had it composed and written:[32]

4498 'Henry, duke and lord of the English and the Normans, greetings to his dear son Henry, king of the empire. Know that Thomas, Archbishop of Canterbury, has reconciled himself to me according to my wishes. I therefore command that he and all his people, lay and lettered, who left the country because of him, should have peace, and that they should have all their property throughout my realm, with nothing held back; also that the Archbishop and his people should hold securely in all peace and honour all lands, churches, and other holdings just as they held them three months before he and his left England. Call together therefore the oldest and most ancient knights that you can find in the fief of Saltwood;[33] see that whatever they shall swear to be due from the whole of that fief to the archbishopric is given and delivered to the Archbishop. When you have seen this letter, keep it.' But the holy and intelligent Archbishop gave orders that the letter be copied and shown everywhere to strangers just as much as to friends: this 'keep it' struck him particularly. The letter was granted to Saint Thomas at Amboise, but was then delivered to his men at Chinon, with the archbishop of Rouen named as witness. The king dragged them from one place to another as much as he could. He made Saint Thomas go back from Amboise into France, journeying as his messenger on his business. The two of them were to meet at Rouen, where the king was to have 500 marks brought to Thomas, with which he would then be able to pay his debts; it had been definitely arranged that the king was to return to him the value of everything that he had taken from him and his people, and Saint Thomas did not intend to allow any reduction. But the first penny was still in doubt; the king still compelled him to wait and wait. He had taken at least £30,000 out of the archbishopric, besides all that he had managed to get from the estates of all the people who were expelled, for the men of this fief were harshly ransomed and the Archbishop's woods were all laid waste and the timber sold.

4541 The Archbishop's men went to England, taking with them the letter from the Old King to the Young King. They had a sufficient number of copies made, and showed them everywhere. And they collected the noblest men of the honour and took them to the king and the justices. Then these men, when they had been brought into the presence of the king and ought to have spoken on behalf of the Archbishop, went and sat down and refused to say a word. Not one of them would make a stand for his lord. They saw dissimulation all about them, and equals in dissimulation they showed themselves to be.

4551 The king's justices delayed endlessly: the whole archbishopric remained destitute. Before these two men could get seisin of the manors, there was nothing left on them—not an ox nor a cow, capon or hen, horse, pig, sheep, or a full bin of corn. The archbishop and the king were reconciled on St. Mary Magdalene's day in summer; they prolonged the delay in giving him seisin of his property until Martinmas,[34] by which time Ranulf de Broc had ransacked and taken everything.

4561 Which of them will answer for this on the great day of wrath, Ranulf or the king? The covetous then will all die and perish eternally; they will not be able to shelter behind each other any more. None of the damage Ranulf had done was made good—God, who knows all and sees all, will put all to rights. God is so just that he cannot do anything but justice, and he hates all wickedness and must punish it. The travelling justices will not do much good then; he whom none of them can deceive will judge them all. Oh God, how many men are blinded by this world! There is no love in it, no peace, no loyalty, no charity. If I were to gain all the possessions there are in the whole earth, and had them so safe that my son would hold them too when my days were done, none of it would do me any good before God. If I were to buy abbeys or great bishoprics which would raise and exalt me in this world, how ruthlessly would I be accused before God for doing so! An honour is dearly bought, when the price is a death sentence.

CHAPTER EIGHT

Return to England

4581 AS SOON AS SAINT THOMAS had been reconciled to the king, he thought about his flock, his flock of so little faith which had gone astray because of its lord's troubles, and he sent his angel into that country before him to cleanse his path and to take away the mire. He sent John of Salisbury,[1] who held a full synod of the clergy and informed them on behalf of the Archbishop that he absolved them all, clerks and laymen, from their sin of having had communion with excommunicates. The reason was that he did not want to greet with a kiss any clerk or layman who might have had dealings with de Broc's men. At the same time he absolved the monks of the monastery who had had any connection with them. He wanted to be able to kiss his own people without hindrance.

4596 When Saint Thomas was about to go to England, King Henry was supposed to meet him at Rouen, to have the money handed over to him as he had promised. He had the following letter[2] delivered to him there: I will read it to you, if you would like to listen:

4601 'Henry, king of the English, duke and lord of the Normans, greetings to Thomas, Archbishop of Canterbury. I hear that Louis, king of France, has summoned his whole host from every part of his empire; he intends to go into the Auvergne to overcome my people, to destroy my vassals and to lay waste my lands. My friends in France have taken care to inform me of this, and the Auvergnats have sent to ask me to go to their help. I ought to go to my rendezvous with you at Rouen, but you must see that I cannot do so. I am therefore sending to you a clerk who has my full confidence: John of Oxford, and I have ordered him to escort you to that country.[3] And I have sent word by him to the young English king, Henry, my eldest son, to tell him that you are to hold your property in peace and security. If there is anything amiss with your business, my son will see that you have redress. My son and I keep hearing news of your delay—perhaps it is not true, but in my opinion you would do well to make haste.' This letter was written at Loches; King Henry witnessed it himself. When Saint Thomas saw it, he got ready for his journey, took leave of the French, and went to England. John of Oxford went with him and was his escort.

4626 Those three prelates who did not love the Archbishop[4] were very anxious when they heard that he was coming back. They went to Canterbury to put their heads together with Sir Ranulf de Broc, and to incite him to make himself master of the Archbishop and his people. So they made his knights and soldiers arm, and took them to Dover by the sea. They had the harbours searched, watched and guarded, so that if the Archbishop tried to come ashore there, they would be ready for him, and able to hinder him, to plunder his men, search his boxes, and take all the letters he had been able to get from Rome; they did not mean to leave him a single one. And so these three prelates had the ports watched—what an evil welcome they were preparing for their father. And in order to make themselves stronger for their great treachery, they added Sír Reginald de Warenne[5] to their number, and Gervase of Cornhill,[6] a man who had never loved him, and Ranulf de Broc. All three of them swore by Mary's son that if they met the Archbishop, he should die.

4646 News of all this reached the Archbishop, for his friends heard about it and told him. He was not at all disheartened, but did feel grief and sorrow for his country and for the free men who had helped him in his exile. He longed to see his country, and to bring back his people with him, exiled by King Henry for six years, and to guide them. He went to Wissant,[7] and walked on the shore to observe the weather and to refresh himself.

4656 Then the dean of Boulogne, called, I believe, Milo,[8] came to bring him a message.

'My lord,' he said, 'I have not come to ask for a passage with you, but to bring a message from my lord, the Count of Boulogne,[9] who sent me here. This is what my lord says to you: that you should keep a careful lookout; you have numerous enemies, all armed; they are keeping a vigilant watch for you at every port on the other side. If you land there you will be cut to pieces or taken to a great fortress and thrown into prison.'

4666 'Fair son', said Saint Thomas, 'I can truthfully declare that even if I were to be cut all to pieces, it would not deter me from completing the journey I have begun, no, not for fear of death or for any other obstacle. No suffering, no dangers, can now restrain me. My church, I know, has wept for her shepherd too long—seven years she has wept for him, night and day. But I now ask my people, if ever I have been a friend to them, to carry me to my church if I am not able to go there alive, if indeed I depart so suddenly from this world. And have my books taken there with me too; if ever I did anything for them that might please them, let them honour me there for what I possess. Nothing more can be given to a man at the end than the thing he most desires, if it may be granted to him.'[10]

4681 When the Archbishop learned that the three men who had so often attacked him were at Dover,[11] he gave the Pope's letter suspending and excommunicating these three prelates to a foot servant and ordered him to cross the sea: he went at once. He reached Dover and found the bishops; they had finished saying their hours, and he addressed the archbishop, saying:

4688 'My lord, I am the Pope's messenger; he sends you by me such greetings as you deserve. Here, read this letter which he has sent you. Hurry up, you are delaying the business of Rome! You are cut off from all appeal and from your divine calling.' Then he turned to the other two and said: 'Take this, my lords. I have a copy of the letter, you will not escape that way. It expels you from the community of the church.' He handed them the letter. When they discovered in it that they were indeed cut off from their calling, they turned pale with grief and anger. Ranulf de Broc very nearly killed the servant, but he could not find him, for God hindered him.

4701 Robert the treasurer also landed at Dover, and was arrested because he had no letter from the king, and had come into England without permission. He had gone, he said, on the primate's business, having been in a hurry to take his cross to meet him.[12]

'Is he coming?' they asked.

'Yes', said Robert, 'indeed he is.'

'But you ought to have managed your journey more sensibly', they said; 'you should have brought a guarantee from some other lord.' And they at once made the treasurer promise to leave again on the next tide if the wind was right. Saint Thomas had received King Henry's firm peace, to return to the country, to have his rights back; if it had been truly sincere and free from deception, they would not have insulted and dishonoured his people —but the impediment quickly made itself apparent.

4716 Saint Thomas went aboard his boat next day; God gave him a good wind, and he landed at Sandwich. He avoided Dover because of the watch being kept there, and stayed at Sandwich, which was his own; huge crowds of his people went there to meet him. But when the three king's men were told that he had landed, they were delighted. They and their men took up their arms, as the three prelates had advised, and set out towards the Archbishop. When John of Oxford saw them coming towards the Archbishop with their weapons, he was extremely worried, for he was well aware that their purpose was rash and wicked, and he also knew that the king would be very much blamed if Thomas the Archbishop suffered any harm. So he went up to them without a moment's delay and told them about the agreement between the king and the baron. He spoke to them as from the king and ordered them by name to do nothing but good to him and his, otherwise the king would be accused of treachery. They must go to him, he told them, without their weapons. They laid them down when he explained this to them, and went and spoke to the Archbishop. They said that he had brought the king's enemy with him, and had disobeyed the king's orders. They said this because of Sir Simon, archdeacon of Sens and a native of that town. He was a tall man, handsome and noble, who had made the journey to see his relations. The king's men wanted to make him swear an oath to hold fast to their king against every other person—they did not except the Pope or anyone else. But Saint Thomas did not want him to pledge fealty, lest all the clergy in the kingdom should have to do so as well.[13] They could not make him do anything against his will, as there were such crowds of his own people gathered there with him. He would not do anything for them, and so they went away again, and the holy Archbishop went to his own city. He was very glad indeed to do so, for he had longed to be there again. The monks and the people gave him a most affectionate welcome, going out to meet him in a great procession.

4756 All the rest of his days he lived a life of sanctity, striving to serve his Lord as much as he could. He took care of widows and orphans and poor people, and gave them clothes, food, shoes, and money; he felt that there were not enough of such people coming to him. No one could turn him from the path of righteousness—he even took from the king's clerks the churches that they had usurped, and gave them back to those who had lost them, and he stood firmly by what was right. He knew very well that he would have to die for righteousness.

4766 Soon after his return from across the sea, he decided that he would not stay for long in his diocese without going to speak with the king of the land, but first of all he sent a messenger ahead of him, a monk called Richard,[14] who ruled the church at Dover. He found the Young King at Winchester.[15] The barons of the country were assembled there, with deans, archdeacons, beneficed clergy and abbots, at the suggestion of the three men who were cut off from the community and of Geoffrey the Married Man.[16] Six churches in the kingdom were without a pastor,[17] and that is why these people—the princes, the earls, and many of the barons—were gathered together then, so as to choose pastors for these posts. From there they were to cross the sea without delay. They were now going to choose men to fill these posts, by the advice of the four men you heard me mention, and they had no intention of summoning any archbishop or primate to assist them, nor, as I will not conceal, did they mean to send for any of the several bishops who would, they knew, wish to take a loyal stand. They did not want the bishop of Winchester, nor Sir Bartholomew, bishop of Exeter, nor that good and noble man, Roger of Worcester, nor yet the bishop of Ely,[18] who for his part was not at all anxious to be present.

No honest man should put his hand to a consecration of this kind. No bishop ought to be ordained anywhere, however many bishops may have assembled, without the primate's approval; this is laid down in canon law. Should the need arise, he may be consecrated by three bishops, but he must not be raised to that rank without the primate's orders. And if a bishop is to be ordained in some country, then the bishops of that kingdom should be sent for, and those who are not able to attend must send messengers with letters making it clear whether they agree to this consecration or not. If a bishop, priest, or deacon is chosen and elevated by a prince, he must be degraded. If anyone has held secular appointments, and by means of them obtains divine office, he must be removed from the community and entirely deposed. I cannot perceive anyone, clerk or lay, who obeys canon or civil law—the very worst offenders are the men in orders. They are afraid of losing their appointments, and so have submitted utterly to the lay power. They bow before the wind, whatever quarter it comes from. Sons of Jesus, indeed! no, they are degenerate, they are not going to get themselves crucified for God just yet if they can help it. They would be most reluctant to let go of anything they had hold of; they are not sprung from heaven, their look is not turned that way—they are made of earth, and they stoop down towards it.

4816 It is the duty of bishops to guide all men. They must be good men, good clerks, born in marriage. A good graft onto a good stock must bear good fruit, and I see clearly that a good scion grafted onto a bad stock bears bad fruit. If a man tends an evil tree, then he must eat evil fruit.

4821 The devil has blinded the kings and princes. A man who has a bad father, has a bad inheritance. One whose leader is weak is often beaten; when a son does so to his father, order is turned upside down, the sky lies under the earth, there is not a star to be seen.[19] When the king appoints a pastor he ought to choose one to whom he can commit his soul and body; if he deliberately selects such a man as will soon alter, if he sets a pure emerald in lead,[20] then I can blame none but himself. A man ought to give holy church a pastor who is so honest that he can honourably bow his head to him. Holy church is the bride of the sovereign Lord, and if she be given an unfit director, then dishonour is done both to God and to his bride.

4836 The Archbishop's messenger arrived at Winchester, but found the door of the room sternly forbidden to him, for both clergy and laymen were afraid he might be bringing some unprofitable letter with him, one which might suspend some of them. The messenger spoke with great discretion: he said that he had not brought any harmful message, and that the primate loved both the king and the king's people dearly. And so he managed to gain admission to the Young King's presence. He bowed low to him and spoke humbly:

4846 'Thomas', he said, 'Archbishop of Canterbury, legate of the see of Rome, primate of the whole empire, greets King Henry, lord of England. You have already heard this from others, my lord king, but I have written to you about it none the less, as I wished you to hear it from myself: that God the merciful has by his grace reconciled your father, who was offended with me, and myself, and has bound us in concord, peace, and love. But I realise that there are several people who are angry about this, and are trying to make trouble for me with you, and to undo and cancel the love and peace. They say that I want to take away your crown. No! so help me God whom all men must serve, so may God bring me to heaven's bliss, I would gladly have won for you more kingdoms than you have already, with my own flesh, with my own blood, as long as God should not blame me for it—so may the Holy Trinity help me at the last. And how should I possibly be aiming at your harm or dishonour, when, as I am bound to do, I hold you to be my king and lord, and the heir and inheritor of the whole realm? and when I love you as I do with loyal affection more than any other man save my lord the king who appointed me to this honour? But I do grieve bitterly in my heart that it was not I who placed the gold crown on your head, according to the dignity of our mother church. And so I have written to ask of your goodness to allow me to discuss other matters with you than this sad error.'

4876 Richard delivered his message well, but the Young King's advisers recommended that he should not at present see the Archbishop. Sir Geoffrey Ridel swore positively that the Old King had told him his wishes about this, that he did not want him to have to talk with this man who was trying to disinherit him of his kingdom, if he could, and to take his crown off his head.

4884 Then he sent two knights to the Archbishop: Thomas de Tournebu,[21] I have heard one of them called; and Jocelin[22] went to him on the king's behalf. He forbade him to set foot in any of the king's strongholds, any town, burgh, or castle; if he were seen in any of them, he would have reason to regret it. (The Archbishop had already travelled to London; he was on his way to see the king and was staying at Southwark.[23])

4891 'What', said Saint Thomas, 'have you renounced allegiance to me?'

'No, certainly not', said Jocelin. 'But the king has sent you this message because you have acted against him so often. You are trying to do away with the laws and customs of his realm, and to take the crown from the Young King; you take armed knights up and down his land, and bring clerks from foreign countries into it; you have cut his prelates off from their function. King Henry requires you to absolve them, now. In this matter and in others you have done him great wrong.' Then the baron could hold his peace no longer, but answered,

4902 'It is not right, I have never seen it set down, that what has been done by a superior can be undone by an inferior—all the more then, what is done, confirmed or commissioned by the Pope cannot lawfully be annulled by anyone lower than himself.' Then these lunatics shouted at him,

4907 'If you don't obey the king's orders, he will make you pay for it, and dearly, too!' (This whole design had been thought up and organised by the three prelates who were cut off from their calling.) The baron answered them perfectly politely, and said that if the bishops of London and of Salisbury would go to him and would swear to stand fast by peace and the rights of holy church, he would undertake and bear the heavy burden of doing this; if he could rely upon the advice of the king, of Roger, bishop of Worcester,[24] and of the other bishops with whom he ought to consult, he would, in the Pope's honour, behave to them in all kindness and humility; they should be most dear to him. Then Jocelin said to him,

4921 'Since you still refuse to absolve the king's prelates, he now forbids you to enter his burghs, his cities, towns and castles; you enter them at your peril. Go and do your work at Canterbury!'

'If I am unable', the saint said to him, 'to go and advise and take care of churches and parishes, then I cannot do my work.' The baron understood clearly that words of this kind meant that he would very soon die a martyr's death.

4931 Then he commended the Londoners and their city to God, the salvation of good men, and came away. Many a miracle has God done at the place where he stayed—health and strength have returned there to the blind, to cripples, to deaf men and dumb, and to lepers. He commended himself to God, and set off. As he went he confirmed children in towns and burghs, in the middle of the road, wherever he was travelling. Wherever people brought them to him, he would get down off his horse;[25] nowhere did he find it a hardship to serve God. He delighted in his service. There is no need to light up[26] all the places where he stood to confirm children—we can go and see the chapels that have been built there. There God makes the blind see, the deaf hear, the dumb speak, he cleanses the lepers and makes the dead arise and walk.

4946 In this manner Saint Thomas returned to his see. He stayed within his archbishopric all the remainder of his life; he had pity on the poor wherever he saw them, and worked night and day to serve God. He knew that his martyrdom was coming; he had spoken about it.

CHAPTER NINE

Martyrdom

4951 ON CHRISTMAS DAY, after preaching, he expelled Robert de Broc from holy church (he had recently been guilty of such rudeness to him as to cut off, in his presence, the tail of one of his packhorses[1]), and others who had acted wrongly towards him. He also spoke to the people about the bishop of London, and him of Salisbury, whom they called Jocelin, and about the archbishop of York, who had on his own authority withdrawn from the church of Holy Trinity its great privilege of the anointing of kings; also about Ranulf de Broc who had done him so much harm and had imprisoned so many of his men. Then he cursed all those who had been the means of his falling out with the king and who had unjustly brought him or should ever in future bring him into trouble with his protector.

4966 'Christ Jesus curse them all!' he said, and threw the candle down upon the paved floor as a sign that their memory should be erased from the book and they themselves expelled from the realm to which the good are called.

4971 When Roger of Pont l'Evêque learned that he had been excommunicated[2] and set apart, he would not make amends or ask for forgiveness, for his heart was evil, full of arrogance and presumptuous pride; the devil had enthroned himself within him. The other prelates, however, his two companions, Gilbert Foliot and Jocelin, did wish to make atonement and to make to their Archbishop those reparations which were justly due; they acknowledged between themselves how wrong they had been. But this man Roger of Pont l'Evêque made them go astray, made them persist in acting against God and against reason; he wanted helpers for his evil plans.

4984 'Don't', he said, 'don't, I beg you, adopt that course, lest your religion should change you;[3] he could so easily turn you about and cheat you. But I have got £10,000 in my treasury; I will spend every one of them, I promise you, to bring Thomas's pride to a fall. He won't be able to do much against me. Now, we will cross the sea and go to the king on the other side; he has supported us so far and he will go on supporting us and our cause against that man. As long as you don't weaken, he will finish him off. Do you know what he will do if you desert him? If you change now and go over to his enemy, you will never enjoy his affection again, however long you live, you will never recover his good will. And he will say that you are running away from right reason. If he does justice upon you, you will lose everything you possess. Then what will you be able to do? Where will you go and beg? And if you stand fast by the king, what else is there that Thomas can do to you? He has passed a sentence on you which cannot be binding because it is not based upon the truth.'

5006 And so he cajoled and persuaded them, and they agreed to go with him. They reached the boat, and put to sea. Roger of Pont l'Evêque could not hide his feelings; he exclaimed,

'Thomas, Thomas, how you will regret making me cross the sea! I am going to get an uncomfortable pillow ready for your head.'

5011 As soon as they had landed, they sent the king the letter from the Pope by which they had lost the exercise of their profession. When the king saw it, he was very angry; he struck his hands together and exclaimed against it vehemently. He went away into his room, white with fury, and said that he had brought up evil men and cared for them, he had given his bread uselessly to an evil people, not one of those nearest him took any share in his griefs. All this terrified his people. 'Why', they said, 'does the king distress himself so dreadfully? If he were to see his sons or his wife being buried, and all his lands in flames, burning, he ought not to grieve like this. If he has heard anything, he ought to have said what it was. Besides, one ought not believe everything one hears. We are ready to carry out anything he orders, to assault and batter down cities and castles, to risk our bodies and our souls as well. He is wrong to complain to us, when he will not say what it is.'

5031 'A man', the king said to them, 'who has eaten my bread, who came to my court poor, and I have raised him high—now he draws up his heel to kick me in the teeth! He has shamed my kin, shamed my realm; the grief goes to my heart, and no one has avenged me!' Then the whole court stirred and murmured; they began to blame themselves severely and to utter fierce threats against the holy Archbishop. Several men started to bind themselves together by oath to take swift vengeance of the king's shame.

5041 When they had crossed the sea, the three companions made straight for Bur.[4] They found the king there and fell at his feet and begged his forgiveness, lamenting and grieving before him, groaning and weeping in sorrow and affliction. Then King Henry's manner quite changed: he told the bishops to get up onto their feet and asked them why they were so unhappy. Archbishop Roger spoke first—he knew all about scheming and wickedness!

5051 'My lord king', he said to him, 'we ought indeed to grieve; and I am able to talk about it and explain it, but no one may speak to these two others, or he too will lie under the same sentence that Thomas laid on them after he crossed the sea. Thomas has excommunicated everyone[5] who was with your son at his consecration, and all those also who approved of it.'

'Then by the eyes God sees with', exclaimed the king, 'I am not excepted, for it has my approval.'

5061 'If my lord', said the archbishop, 'you have to

share in our sufferings, it will be the easier for us to bear it. He is forcing your free men to leave holy church and your bishops to lie under excommunication. And he does not mean to stop at that—since he returned to the country, he has gone about your land strongly reinforced with men, he has knights and soldiers with him, all armed and ready, in the fear that he may be exiled again; he is seeking assistance everywhere, to make himself stronger. We do not mind, we do not complain, that our loyalty in your service has led to our expending so much of our own resources and to our weariness and suffering—as long as we are not cut off from your love—but we do complain at his doing us this injustice, disgracing and dishonouring us as if we were evildoers. You would certainly not be blamed if you were to follow a different policy. But wait until he feels secure; then you will be able to take your revenge without any disturbance.'

5081 The letter from the Pope cutting off these three prelates from their calling was brought forward and was read out in audience and listened to by everyone. Then indeed ill-will blazed out everywhere, with insults and threats against Saint Thomas. Christmas day this year was on a Friday; it was on the eve, Thursday, that this council and God's enemies met together and swore the death of God's friend. They thought they could bring him down, but it was they who reaped the disgrace. They swore now on holy relics and pledged each other that wherever in the world they might find him, they would pull his tongue down past his chin and dig both his eyes out of his head; neither church nor altar nor season should protect him. This room at Bur has had a strange destiny—many are the bitter tidings it has heard. It was here that Rainild was given by oath to Harold,[6] here that the army of England[7] took its oath to the Bastard, and here too the death of Saint Thomas was *[5100]* pledged and sworn. All the best men of the court pledged each other to accomplish this dreadful act of cruelty. But their names shall not be set down in my book, for they have repented and God has forgiven them;

my writing shall not shame them in the eyes of the world. The best, the bravest, and the wisest of the court, Englishmen and Normans, were inspired by the deceiving traitor;[8] and they went to the ports, one here, another there, to Dieppe and Winchelsea,[9] Barfleur and Wissant. They all wanted to cross the sea if they could, so as to keep watch and ward over the English ports and prevent anyone from going to England and telling the Archbishop what had happened, thus enabling him to get away. Perhaps if they had got across then, they would have behaved differently from the way they did in fact later behave, but at this time they had neither good wind nor good weather. God did not hate them so much as to let them be involved in this, nor had the devil such power over them.

5121 But the four traitors and enemies of God, whom God hated because of their evil lives—Hugh de Morville, William de Tracy, Reginald FitzUrse, and a fourth, Richard the Breton[10]—left the court. Roger of Pont l'Evêque went with them and did all he could to incite them to commit this evil deed[11]—Thomas was distressing and troubling the whole kingdom; if he were dead, so he said, peace would be restored; he took upon himself the guilt of anything that they might do. He composed and repeated to them the argument and all the expressions that they afterwards used to the Archbishop in his room, and he gave each of the four men 60 marks. Thus the blood of the righteous was bought and sold, thus Judas the covetous went to the Jews.

5136 The very men whose duty it should have been to advise the king better, to turn him from his evil path and set him in the right way, are the ones who had Saint Thomas cut down and killed; it is they who should be accused and blamed, and whom the king ought to banish far from his presence. If he really repents, he must never go near them, for their advice has caused him grievous harm and he is much blamed for trusting them. They have never recommended to him anything but what he wanted—and how disloyal is counsel that merely toadies inclination.

5146 Two of these four men crossed the sea to Dover, and two to Winchelsea. They had no trouble finding a boat, nor with the crossing, the wind, or the weather—everything fell out as they wished. They all went to Saltwood and met there. Sir Ranulf de Broc had gone to meet them; he took them to the castle and lodged them there. Candles had been lit, but he had them put out, and they talked all night, discussing what they would do. Anyone who was allowed in, knew all about their plans. In the morning the knights of that district were summoned, and were told to follow on, ready and well equipped with arms to fulfill the king's business. Sir Ranulf de Broc had already sent out these orders; they had all been summoned by proclamation to the rendezvous with these men.

5161 They arrived in Canterbury on the fifth day of Christmas,[12] when people had just finished their dinner; it was the day following that upon which the Innocents were beheaded, whom Herod slew in his great cruelty, thinking that in the children he could murder the Deity. The knights and soldiers of the neighbourhood were summoned to avenge the king of England's shame; if anyone were to try to hide the Archbishop or to get him away, they must besiege the church next morning, set fire to it and bring it to the ground. The reeve[13] had proclamation made throughout the city that no one, great or small, whatever he might see, whatever he might hear reported, should dare to offer any resistance; each man that cared about himself or his possessions must be ready to assist the king's work.

5176 These madmen rode into the Archbishop's courtyard and dismounted outside the hall. The Archbishop had by then finished eating and was sitting in his room with his trusted clerks. Even the servants had already got up from the tables.[14] The four men entered the hall alone, except for an archer of Ranulf's whom they brought with them. The seneschal[15] came forward to the foot of the steps to meet them; they exchanged greetings and kisses. The seneschal was a tall, handsome knight, born in that district, rich, and possessed of many fiefs. He had served at the meal and then had dined himself; after that he had gone to the Archbishop's room and said,

5190 'My lord, please might I speak to you for a moment? I have decided to take your advice, my lord, and go to our king's court, and remain there, because you are in such disfavour with the king and his men that I do not dare stay here with you any longer; the king may hold it against me if I do.'

5196 'Of course you have my leave to go, William', he answered. 'I do not want to make you stay here, if you want to go to the king's court.' After which he went away, and coming to the stairs, he encountered the four king's men, and at their orders he then went back into the room.

5201 'My lord', he said, 'there are four young men of the king's knights here'—but he would not say their names—'they want to speak to you on behalf of King Henry.'

'Show them in', the Archbishop replied, and William did so at once.

5206 The four men had agreed what to do: they sat down right in front of Saint Thomas, at his feet, and the archer sat down on the floor behind them. But they did not greet Saint Thomas, or speak to him—nor did the Archbishop, who was talking with the clerks, speak to them. I do not know whether the baron did this deliberately, not wanting to greet them immediately they came in, as they would not speak, to tell him why they were there, or whether it was because he was so intent on his discussion with the monks and clerks. The holy man leaned on his elbow towards one of the monks; then sat upright and looked straight at the barons—and yet he looked compassionately at the four men. Some say that he named one of them, William, and greeted him, but none of the others, by name. Then the four madmen looked downwards; they did not receive his greeting or return it—he who was guiding them hated their salvation! They exchanged glances among themselves. Then the baron began to feel more than a little surprised at their silence. Some say that Reginald, the other three being silent, said hypocritically, 'God be your aid!' and at this the holy man turned redder than the choicest scarlet cloth, for he knew very well that this was meant as an insult.

5231 Then, in a somewhat angry manner, Reginald said:

'We have brought a message across the sea for you from the king. Are you going to listen to it in private, or do you want all your people to hear it?'

'Just as you wish', answered the baron.

'Oh no, as it shall please you!' they said.

'No, as you please', said the baron, and they began arguing about it. Then Saint Thomas sent all his people, except the man on guard at the door, into the larger room, till he had heard what they had come about. But after that Saint Thomas said,

5241 'Never mind the door; this ought not to be kept secret. Quick, bring back all the clerks of my privy council, I do not want to be parted from them.' And so they came back in, but I cannot give their names. If they had not returned so promptly, if the traitors had had any weapons or a knife, they would have killed him between them, for they have subsequently admitted this. They were on the point of striking him down and killing him with the shaft of the cross, but God averted it. Then Reginald said,

5251 'The king has sent you word across the sea: he had made peace with you and declared you forgiven, and you had done the same to him, but you have not kept the agreement. You have entered his kingdom improperly, going to his castles with your vassals in arms. Also you have excommunicated and cut off from God his men who were present at his son's coronation, and an archbishop of his who had occasion to go to him, and two of his bishops with whom he needed to talk. You are trying to bring down and do away with the customs of the realm, and to take away the Young King's crown. Now the king wants to know if you will go to his court to make amends before him and undergo judgment.'

5264 'I have done', he replied, 'everything for the king that my duty demands; I cannot recollect anything left undone. And I have no wish', he said, 'to bring down the king's crown; I would sooner help him to gain lawful possession of three more. I came into his land with his full permission, and my lord has no right to bring accusations against me if my vassals and my tenants escort me on my way. I am fully prepared to make amends to him at his court and in any other place, if I have done any wrong. He, though, has forbidden me to go into his burghs and cities, his towns and castles; I would enter them at my peril. The king has released holy church from her rights! The suspension did not originate with me, but with Pope Alexander, because of the anointing of the Young King (God grant him his blessing!), which they performed wrongly and unreasonably, and for which they refused to make atonement.'

5281 'But it was at your instigation', Reginald answered, 'that the king's three prelates were excommunicated, and so the king wants them freed, he wants you to absolve them at once, just as it was you who suspended and excommunicated them.'

5286 'I do not deny', he said, 'that it may have been at my instigation, but they shall get no help or relief from me. Let all three of them go at once to our Pope, for they have fallen, and most justly, into his nets; I do but obey him and carry out his orders.'

'Very fine threats!' said the sons of Satan. 'You will find yourself under better guard than you are used to; you won't get away out of this, as you did before.'[16] Saint Thomas was unshaken, undismayed:

'No one', he said, 'shall ever force me to leave; I will not be driven out of the country for any man.'

'What', they said to him, 'would you not go for the king's sake?'

5298 'No', he said, 'I shall never cross the sea again. I will never leave, not for anyone. You will find me here.' These words made them very angry. 'You have no right', he said, 'to bring me such a message. My lord the king is a man of honour and loyalty, he would not send me anything of this kind; he will never ratify it.'

'He will though', they said; 'we have every right to deliver it.'

'I', said Saint Thomas, 'have many complaints to make of his men. They hold our churches by violence and in sin,[17] they have beaten my men, cut off my packhorse's tail, and have violently made off with my barrels and my wine which my lord the king had sent on its way to me.'[18]

5311 'If the vassals of the lord of the realm', said Reginald, 'have behaved wrongly towards you in any way, why did you not begin by reporting it to the king, who would have taken counsel with the barons and put matters right?' The saint flung back his head—

'If I had any need to summon witnesses', he said, 'you were there yourself, Reginald, and so were 200 knights, when the king granted me permission to avenge the wrongs done to holy church. I will right them myself; it is for me to do it; it belongs to my calling.' They turned red at that, like blazing fires:

5322 'What', they said, 'did the king give into your hand all the men who crowned his son? And everything they did, as you know, was done by him. In our very hearing, you make him out to be a traitor! You dishonour him, just as you have always done.'

5327 'No I do not', said Saint Thomas. 'I do not think him a traitor; I do not seek to shame him—on the contrary, I long for him to have very great honour. But he did grant me permission to do justice on them, on the day when God set love and peace between us two. I complained to him about them by name, and he granted me—200 men heard me—permission to take my full rights of them. He has nothing to do with me or with my clerks; I will punish them, as it is my business to do. I cannot go running to court for every offence; no, I am a priest, and as such I will exercise divine justice upon those who offend against holy mother church.'

5339 'Threats!' they said, 'threats! They will be paid for, if you do not absolve the men under sentence.'

'Your threats', he replied, 'cannot make you any the more terrible, if you really come from the king. You may strike here, at my naked neck, not the flimsiest blade shall protect it from you', and he put his hand to his neck.

5345 They went away then. 'There is more to it than threats!' they shouted, and then most basely they defied the holy Archbishop. They summoned everyone to leave at once, in the king's name; they would pay for it if they lingered. And they ordered the monks whom they found there to keep him securely, in the king's name, for if he escaped he would be required at their hands, they would have to produce him.[19] The saint arose; he had heard and noted their defiance, and he followed the knights to the door of the room after they had uttered it, for he heard it clearly, and called after them,

5358 'Hugh, what have you said? Answer me!' But they made no reply and went away. If he could have had his wish, they would have murdered him then and there.

Saint Thomas came back and sat down on his bed; he became as it were totally caught up in the spirit. Then John of Salisbury said to him,

'My lord, you have invariably gone against our advice, and done what you had determined on in your own heart.'

'What do you want me to do, Sir John?' asked the baron.

'You ought to have summoned your council', he said, 'when the knights came in here to speak with you. All they want is a pretext for your death. But no one can release you from your own obstinacy.'

5371 'We must all die', Saint Thomas told him. 'You will never find me flinching from what is right for fear of death. And I want to endure death for the love of God; they cannot be any readier to strike than my heart is to suffer martyrdom.'

'We', said Master John, 'are not so well prepared that we wish to be handed over to death, for we lie in weakness and sin. I see no one but you choosing to die.'

'God's will be done', said Saint Thomas.

5381 Meanwhile the four knights were outside arming themselves; they took off their tunics and girded on their steel blades (for they had come in full armour, on their warhorses). They were soon ready for their most evil task. There were plenty of people to go and tell the Archbishop about it.

'My lord', the monks said to him, 'go into the church; they are singing vespers now;[20] you ought not to miss it. These knights want to take you and cut you to pieces.'

'You will not see me letting that alarm me', he said. 'I shall wait here for whatever God may here send me.'

5391 When they had got their weapons, the four young knights went to the doors of the hall, but they could not get in, for the doors had been securely barred behind them earlier on. Then they started battering at the doors, because they wanted to get hold of the saint and slaughter him. But they could not break the doors down; so then Robert de Broc, expert in contriving evil, said,

5398 'Follow me, my lords, free knights, I will get you in another way.' They went past the kitchen and into the orchard. There was a closed gallery by the door of the room, which gave directly onto the garden; it had been there many a long day, and at present the stairs had been removed for repairs to be done. The carpenters had gone to dinner, and the knights made their way to this gallery. Robert de Broc got into the rooms by this route, and he brought the knights in up ladders. They took with them the tools belonging to the workmen who were making the stairs, hatchets and a double-edged axe, so as to break down any doors they might find shut. Saint Thomas's people heard them coming, and began to scatter like sheep pursued by wolves, just as the apostles did when they saw Pilate's men arrest Jesus—who had come into the world that he might die to establish his church. Not one of all his servants stayed with him, except a few of his clerks—there were brave men among them—and Master Edward Grim,[21] and some monks, I do not know how many. These men laid hold of Saint Thomas, who was still sitting down awaiting death and the end of his days—for ever since he had come back from his exile across the sea he had said, in the hearing of several whom I have heard speak about it, that he would die that same year, he was certain of it. There were now only two days of the year left; the third, in which he was to meet his end, was all but gone. On Christmas day itself many who had gone to hear him preach heard him speak about this:

5428 'I have come here', he said, 'to suffer death amongst you'. Now the day had come when this was to be accomplished. In his life and in his death he was a most glorious martyr. And at the end of his sermon, too, he spoke prophetically to one of his clerks, Alexander of Wales,[22] in many people's hearing, saying,

5434 'There is indeed one martyr here, St. Alphege;[23] if it please God, you will soon have another.' That is why he stayed where he was and refused to run away; he was calm and perfectly ready for death. He thought that they would not dare to attack him in the church, and therefore stayed where he was, not wanting to avoid death. But God wanted him to fall in a more glorious place, and so they now began to lead him towards the church. But they had almost to carry him there by force—you would have seen some of them dragging him along, others pushing him.[24] Their only route, however, lay through the solid wall or through locked doors, if they wanted to get by. There was one room, adjacent to the others, through which there was a more private way to the cloisters, but it was at that time shut fast with a large bolt.[25] Very dismayed were the monks when they found their way blocked in every direction. One of them went to this door and grasped the bolt in both his hands—and God worked a miracle: when he tried to move the bolt, it fell off into his hands as if it had been stuck on with a little glue. The monk opened the door and hurried them all through it. Then, whether he liked it or not, they took him to the church, while he was waiting voluntarily for death. Some pulled him, some pushed, and they got a good way along inside the cloister. They stopped twice, though, in the cloister, for as soon as the saint managed to touch the ground and get both his feet down firmly, he pushed them all away and began to protest—

5464 'Why are you dragging and pulling me along?' he said. 'Leave me alone!' Then they took hold of him and carried him into the church.

No sooner had the monks carried him into the church than the knights entered the cloister, with their hauberks on, their swords in their hands, accompanied by one Hugh, called Mauclerc,[26] a clerk of Robert de Broc's, full of wickedness. On came these four to begin their crime. (Four other knights[27] followed them in the distance; this man Hugh went with them into the church, but the others did not go in, for the sons of the devil encountered them on their way back through the cloister.) Some of the monks shut the doors against them.

5477 'Open the doors', said Saint Thomas, who was waiting for these men. 'On holy obedience', he said, 'I command you to open them. Let them fulfill their purpose; they are blind and ignorant. I will not go a step further as long as you keep the doors shut. No one ought to make the house of God, the true Lord, into a castle, a fortress, a tower, but we clerks who are his servants and ministers ought always to be its defence and make our bodies shields against the evildoer.' He himself unbarred and opened the doors, and thrust back the people who had collected there to see what would happen.

5488 'What are you frightened of?' he asked.

'Look', they said, 'here come the armed knights.'

'I will go to them', he said.

'You will not!' they answered. They compelled him to go as far as the northern staircase,[28] trying to get him to the protection of the holy relics.

'My lords', he said to the monks, 'I insist that you let me go. This is none of your business; let God see to it. Go up into the choir and sing your vespers.'

5496 The servants of Satan were inside the church now, drawn swords in their right hands. They had the hatchets in their left hands; the fourth man was carrying the axe. There was a pillar there, supporting the vaulting, which blocked their view of the holy Archbishop.[29] Three of them went to one side of the pillar, demanding 'the traitor to the king'; Reginald went to the other side, where he found a monk and asked where the Archbishop was. At that the saint spoke to him:

5505 'If you are looking for me, Reginald, you have found me.' Saint Thomas had not heard the word 'traitor', but stood still and listened at the word 'archbishop', and went down the steps towards Reginald.

'If it is me you want, Reginald', he said, 'I am here', and Reginald grabbed him by the edge of his cloak.

'Reginald', said the good priest, 'I have done you many kindnesses; for what purpose do you come armed against me in holy church?'

5513 'You will find out!' said Reginald FitzUrse, and he jerked him forwards so that he stumbled. 'You are a traitor to the king! Come away with us.' He meant to drag him out of the holy church. I can well believe that it annoyed Saint Thomas to be pushed and pulled about by this Reginald; he gave him a shove that sent him right back, and tugged the edge of his cloak out of his hands.

5521 'Leave this building, you worthless man!' said the tonsured saint. 'I am no traitor, I deserve no such accusation.' Reginald paused a moment, then said,

'Get away from here.'

'No, I will not', the saint answered. 'You will find me here, you can achieve your wicked crime here.' The baron went away towards the north aisle and set his back against a pillar. It stood between two altars, the upper one being consecrated to the mother of God, the other in the name of St. Benedict. The frenzied tools of Satan dragged him towards it.[30]

'Absolve the excommunicates!' they said, 'and the men you have suspended and cut off.'

'I will do nothing more for them than I have done already', he said. Then they all of them together threatened him with death.

5536 'I am not afraid of your threats', he said. 'I am ready to suffer martyrdom. But let my people go, do not touch them; do what you have to do to me alone.' At the point of death, the good shepherd did not forget his own. It was just the same with God, when he went at nightfall to pray on the Mount of Olives, and the men who sought him began shouting, 'Where is the Nazarene?' —'You may find me here', God answered them, 'but let all my people go.'

5546 Then the sons of the devil took hold of him and began to tug and pull at him, and tried to heave him up onto William's shoulders, for they wanted to get him out of there, and kill or bind him; but they could not get him away from the pillar. For Saint Thomas was set firm against that Pillar who died on the cross to establish his church, and from this Pillar no one could ever detach him. But now the people's salvation demanded that one man be given over to death, beside the pillar of the church. Those who ought more than any others to have protected holy church, were trying to destroy her and her members, to bring that Pillar and the Head which it supported crashing to the ground. Blood was needed, to wash this blood guilt clean; the head's head had to be offered, to raise the head up again.[31] It was not that God wanted him to be treated so foully; he was testing these wicked men—perhaps they would not dare commit so atrocious a sin within holy church. For there is no one from here to the Orient, however bad a man he may be, who can hear about this crime without horror.

5566 Master Edward Grim had got a tight hold on him; he gripped him round the body when they attacked him and held fast against them all, undismayed; the knights could not make him let go. Clerks, monks, and servants had all fled; Master Edward held him, pull how they might.

'What do you think you are doing?' he cried. 'Are you out of your minds? Think where you are, what season it is. Think of your sin, in raising your hand against your archbishop!' But they did not check, for the sake of the holy season or of the church.

5576 Now indeed Saint Thomas saw his martyrdom approaching. Hands joined before his face, he gave himself to the Lord God, commending himself, his cause, and the cause of the holy church, to the martyr St. Denis, to whom sweet France belongs, and to the saints of the church. William came forward, not to adore God! He had left off his hauberk so as to be unencumbered, and began demanding 'the traitor to the king'. As they could not get the saint out of the church, he struck him hard with his sword on the head, slicing off the top of his tonsure and cutting deeply into his scalp, so that it fell downwards. The sword came down onto his left shoulder, cutting through his cloak and clothes to the skin. It cut Edward's arm almost in two, and at the blow Master Edward released his hold.

5592 'Strike! strike!' he[32] cried; then Sir Reginald FitzUrse struck him, but did not bring him down. Then William de Tracy struck at him again and brained him, and Saint Thomas fell. When the criminals went back to Saltwood that night, they boasted of their great wickedness; William de Tracy said he was sure he had cut John of Salisbury's arm off; that is how we know that it was he who wounded Master Edward. He was not wearing armour, and so came ahead of the others as they pursued Saint Thomas; he was distinctly recognised both by his face and by his voice. He was wearing a green tunic and a two-coloured cloak. When he saw Reginald FitzUrse step back, he struck the saint twice on the head, as I have described.

5606 Then when Richard the Breton saw him struck down and lying stretched out on the paved floor, he gave him a blow which fell slightly athwart the others, and his keen-edged blade hit the stone and broke in two. (The broken-off piece is in the Martyrdom,[33] where people may touch it with their lips.) Although these evil men slashed and struck him so violently, although they hit out at him with all their strength, he uttered no shout, no groan, he did not cry out or exclaim; he did not withdraw hand or foot towards himself, for he rested his whole heart and strength upon God. And just as the Jews, his sons, crucified God for the sake of human sin upon Calvary, in the place where justice corrected crimes, so did this man's sons martyr him for the sake of the clergy in the place where misdeeds are made clean and washed away.

5621 Hugh de Morville had run further on and was driving back the people who had gathered; he was afraid the Archbishop might be taken from them. Perhaps he had come to his senses and took this way of avoiding a share in the crime.

5626 When Herod's knights, Ishmael's children, killed Rachel's son in Jerusalem, they did not cut the crown of his head right off; it was still attached to the flesh and skin of his forehead; you could see the brain laid all open. And then this man Hugh Mauclerc, who had followed them in, put his foot hard down on Saint Thomas's neck, poked the brains out of his head onto the floor with his sword, and shouted to the others,

'Let's go; he won't get up again.'

5635 Anyone who saw the blood and the brains fall and lie mingled on the stone floor might have thought of roses and lilies, for he would have seen the blood showing red among the white brains, and the brains gleaming white against the red blood.

5641 Then the bondslaves of iniquity went away. They went back through the cloisters, grasping their swords and shouting out, 'King's men!' They were knights once, but now they are worthless and detested. They were great men once, but now are fallen into sorrow. Miserable wretches! what have you done? You never gave a thought to God or to the church. Your children's children will bear your shame as long as this world lasts. He who destroys fine men for the sake of animals[34] is fast asleep;

God is up there in heaven; the kingdom goes all awry. For the northern church, in the north aisle, and facing towards the north, did Saint Thomas suffer death. Through his death God has made him glorious and mighty —all Christians turn to him for help and strength, and he brings those in peril on the sea home to their harbours.

5656 While the sons of the devil were committing this dreadful heresy in the holy church, Robert de Broc and others as well stayed behind to pillage the rooms and break open the strongboxes. They took woven stuffs and plate, silver and pure gold; they took his good blade,[35] worth the price of a city, and a ring with a very choice sapphire set in it (he would not have accepted any offer for it; no one ever saw a better), and a great piece of very rich crimson samite; his books were taken and all his writings, and the gold chalice the saint used at mass (many a time they have battered and broken it on their dining table), vestments, clothes, and everything they could find —spoons, cups, goblets of silver and of refined gold, and at least sixty pounds of coined silver; also all his jewels that he kept so carefully and would not show to everyone—and much more, more than I can describe or than any of his men can tell me for certain. Charters, privileges, they *[5675]* had them all taken away. They ransacked Saint Thomas's rooms and all the buildings; they would leave nothing behind them; whatever they found, they took. They took Saint Thomas's horses too, and where they could find his men and his clerks they laid hold on them and their possessions and put them into prison. No such outrage has ever been committed in any place under the rule of law, in any land at peace—nor, all the more, in a land where the king shows mercy to no one. There is no ruler in the world, near or far, who exercises justice more harshly than he does—but I will not speak of this. Even for the sake of dumb beasts, he exacts the severest penalties, killing fine men, torturing many. But God, who punishes wrongdoing in his own good time, would not allow vengeance to be taken for the holy martyr who was killed in holy church.

5691 And so holy church was profaned and desecrated. No matins was sung there, no vespers, no mass; God was not served there, no candles were lit. The doors were shut and the people kept out. Holy church was thus a prisoner all the year long—or all the year but for 10 days. On the fifth day after Christmas she was thrown into prison, and on the fifth day before Christmas she was blessed anew. The tenth was saved, that of the people and that of the days;[36] and the battle between the clerks and the king was brought to an end. For the sake of his tonsured people, the good priest gave his defenceless tonsure to armed men. How spiritual a battle it was on his side, when he offered his tonsure as a shield against swords! Never would he give way to them, not for any blow or injury. Yet he could easily have avoided his death, if he had trusted the cowled brothers, for there are many hiding places in that church. No, he suffered death willingly in the sacred building, and God has rewarded him with great honour in this world. Never has so foul a deed been done in the world, nor one which has done the world so much good. Yet the world will find it has to pay for it, and dearly too. Sooner or later God's wrath will blaze out, for the avenging of this deed is his alone. But God's vengeance does not hurry; it requires that the guilt be atoned for. God neither wills nor desires the soul's damnation. The week is not yet begun in which crime will be both discovered and avenged.

5721 The first ill effect has been the destruction of Normandy, for it was there that the holy man's death was first planned, and it was Normandy's guardian[37] from whom the whole trouble sprang. Through the door which he thought he could shut on that gap, the way has been opened, and God's anger revealed. But God has, I am sure, turned away the wrath which he had prepared for the kingdom and the people, for King Henry has acknowledged that the guilt is entirely his, he has atoned for the whole crime himself, and has given holy church her absolute freedom.

5731 No one could have seen his clerks and his men fleeing, his nephews and relations running into hiding, taking off their good clothes and putting on poor ones, without feeling his flesh shiver with compassion. Every one of them was sure he would die.

Then the devil's children went away in joy and delight, rejoicing over the wicked thing they had done. May God enable them to atone for it! But they will never be loved, never held dear, by anyone except those who shared in their crime.

5741 The news spread fast; old and young shook with fear as they heard that a new holy martyr lay in the church, dead upon the floor. The monks gathered up his blood and brains and put them in jars beside his head, outside the tomb. His holy body was carried to the high altar and laid before it; the monks and others watched it all night. The blood that dripped from it was collected.

5749 On the following day a nephew of Ranulf de Broc's went to Canterbury about the body; he was called Robert and was a well-known man, usher to the king. None of the gates or doors were shut against him, for men feared him because of the king. He took two of Saint Thomas's best horses—as for those belonging to his clerks, he took them all. (For Saint Thomas's clerks had fled to the monks for safety with all the rest of the people, taking with them their horses and everything else. Much good it did them! the de Brocs took all they could find, wherever they found it, just as they felt inclined, and his clerks and his men as well, and kept tight hold of it all.) Robert said:

5761 'The land is freed of the traitor who was trying to take away his lord's crown. He ought to be treated as shamefully as possible; he should be thrown into a rubbish pit, or some filthier more stinking place.' Here was a man with little fear of God! 'It is a great blessing', he said, 'that this traitor has been killed; so excellent a deed was never attempted before. If St. Peter had behaved to the king as wrongly as he did, and I had been there, by St. Denis's body! my naked sword would have carved into his brains.' And then he ordered the monks to take up the body and to hide it where neither dark nor fair could see it, or else he would have it shamefully dragged out by horses, or cut in pieces, never to be recovered; it should be thrown into a rubbish pit, flung to the dogs and pigs. The monks were terrified at this, and so they hid and buried him in the crypt.

5778 First, however, they examined his body and his clothes, and discovered that he was not at all fat or stout but was dressed and burdened with the very holiest clothing. On top of his other clothes he had an iron-dark cloak, lined with white lamb's fur, black fastenings, no edging, and under this a handsome white surplice of fine weave; next there was a white lambskin coat—he did not wear ermine or miniver, samite or sendal. This was the outer habit of a regular canon. Under it he wore two jackets made of lamb's fur, both of them short and roomy; they cut these off him with knives. I have seen them subsequently, and know very well to whom they were given.[38] His body and stomach were always very cold, and he was subject to attacks of pain in the side, and that is why he always dressed so warmly—in order to avoid falling ill through cold, and also so that he could get warm again quickly when he had himself flogged. Under these things the baron wore a monk's cowl and woollen shirt, but he had had the skirts and sleeves shortened, because he did not want to reveal his way of life to the world. When the monks saw them, they cried out, 'Look, here is a true monk! Here you can find one!' Then under that he wore a hair shirt next to his skin, arranged so that it could not be seen, and drawers of hair too, right against his bare skin, but with white drawers covering them, made of expensive stuff, because he did not want his way of life generally known.

5806 But these goat hair garments were thickly covered on both sides with minute vermin; they were all over them in crowds and clusters; their attacks on his flesh were such that it was astonishing how he could have endured such punishment. He suffered a far worse martyrdom whilst he lived than he did when they killed him in the church, for then he died at once and was taken into bliss—but all this vermin that had entrenched itself on him tormented him day and night for years.

5816 The monks grieved and rejoiced over him—they grieved to see him cut down, but when they discovered what kind of life he had led, they rejoiced. Yet if they had examined his naked body, they would have found it all cut by whips—on that very day when he was slaughtered, Saint Thomas had received the discipline three times.

5823 Then they buried him with great honour, in the crypt for fear of the de Brocs, lest they should find him—but now it is he that is feared and honoured throughout the world. The first martyrdom was an atonement for the sins he had committed formerly, in secular life; he endured these great torments as a reparation for great delights. The second martyrdom sanctified him; it was through the one that he at last attained the other.

5831 Then the de Brocs seized the archbishopric. That was an evil archbishop for the king to appoint! They set up laws that reflected their own natures; they compelled the priests to sing mass, although it was forbidden; holy church fell into total decay. Ranulf de Broc was head of the archbishopric; whatever he did or undid was always confirmed. He sent all the rents and wealth to the king—all that money could never be put to a good use, obtained as it was by treachery. Once this money should be spent and gone, wasted upon wicked men and upon making war, wrongly gained and wrongly spent, the dice would soon fall differently. It would be double ones now, not double sixes. For no one can rely upon his wealth; no one can put off what is to come by means of Brabançons,[39] or Flemings, Englishmen, or all the French, for God holds the outcome balanced on his little finger; as long as it pleases him, he abides our wrongdoings in patience. The de Brocs will be as the Jews were, who caused God the merciful to be slain—they expected to lose their lands and homes,[40] and now they have all been driven out, they have no fief or inheritance. The de Brocs will meet a far worse fate and find far harsher enemies.

CHAPTER TEN

Triumph of Saint Thomas

5856 THE HOLY MARTYR whose story you have heard was born on St. Thomas's night before Christmas while vespers were singing; and was baptised after vespers; they called him Thomas after the saint. And while vespers were being sung he was carried to the highest heavens. His namesake was killed in the days when holy church was young and growing, and he lies in the east; this Thomas was killed in the north for the sake of his church which was in decay, and he protects the west. They share Christmas and Jerusalem equally between them. Both of them died for the church on earth; both by their deaths gained the kingdom of heaven. They used all their five wits in God's service; they climbed and overcame the five steps. They keep watch over the two parts of the whole world.[1]

5871 This holy man I am telling you about was born on a Tuesday, and it was on a Tuesday that he fled from Northampton; moreover it was also a Tuesday when he crossed the sea, and it was the same day again when he returned from exile—and it was upon a Tuesday that he suffered martyrdom.

5876 Since we have been given a new martyr so recently, Guernes[2] the clerk, born at Pont-Sainte-Maxence, would like to tell you at what date the martyrdom happened—it was eleven hundred and sixty years and ten since God was incarnate in the Virgin.

5881 Saint Thomas is high in favour with Our Lord God, everyone can see it, no need to ask if any disagree.

It is unheard of since the first century that God should demonstrate such love towards any dead man—he does the most mighty miracles for him, day and night. God is here with us upon earth for love of the martyr. He brings the dead to life, makes the dumb speak, the deaf hear, cripples stand up straight, he cures the gouty and the fevered, restores the dropsied and leprous to health, makes the blind see and brings lunatics into their right minds. Kings have sought him in pilgrimage, princes, barons, dukes with their nobles, strangers from foreign countries, speaking many languages, prelates, monks, recluses, crowds of foot travellers; they take phials home with them as a sign of their journey. People bring a cross back from Jerusalem, a Mary cast in lead from Rocamadour, a leaden shell from St. James; now God has given Saint Thomas this phial, which is loved and honoured all over the world. In the likeness of wine and water, God has his blood consumed throughout the world, to save souls; in water and in phials he has the martyr's blood taken all over the world, to cure the sick. It is doubly honoured, for health, and as a sign.[3]

King Henry's Penitence

5906 But one of the most extraordinary things is this: that we see the men who used to hate Saint Thomas mortally, who made trouble for him with King Henry and caused strife between them, who planned and effected his death—we see these very men becoming his vassals, seeking his forgiveness. The king of England himself, who was his enemy, who caused his six-year and more absence from the country, whose anger led his men to go and kill him, went to him in the fourth year in great humility and begged his forgiveness for all that he had done wrong. In the fourth year after the martyr suffered his passion, in the seventh month, called July, and on the 12th day, a Friday, the king went to the martyr to make atonement. In very pressing need, he went to the baron for help.

5921 There is a lepers' hospital near Canterbury, full of sick and diseased people; it is about a league from the great church in which lies the holy body of the spiritual healer who has restored so many sad folk to joy and well being. The king dismounted there, at Harbledown, went into the church and prayed; he asked forgiveness of God for all he had done wrong. For love of Saint Thomas he granted an income of 20 marks to this needy house.[4] And at another hospital a good two leagues from there, one which sheltered poor people, the king behaved well, for he gave it an income of 100 shillings a year.[5] May God bless him, who made him go to that place, and who will make it better than it is at present.[6]

5936 He went on foot as far as St. Dunstan's, the first church he came to inside the town; and together with the prelates who were present he went into the church where he cleansed his spirit by confession, underwent discipline, and punished his flesh. Then he sent the prior to the monastery, asking him to assemble its lords; he would gladly and willingly agree to do all that they should decide upon among themselves as being right for him to do by way of atonement to the martyr. Then he at once had his footwear removed and walked up through the town on the stony ways, barefoot, so as to punish his flesh, and wearing nothing but his underclothing and a rain cloak that he used to go riding in. He wanted to make his peace with God by severe penance.

5951 It is usual to ring a full peal of bells to greet a king, to gather a procession with which to meet him, and to lead him with every honour into the church, but the king ordered all this to be set aside. He wanted to come not as a king but as a beggar. He approached the door humbly, and knelt down; and stayed there a long time weeping and praying. Then he entered the church and went to the Martyrdom, said the *confiteor* and kissed the marble. After that he went to the tomb[7] and made his peace with the martyr.

5961 When the king had prayed there for a long time, lying long in grief and tears, his heart utterly contrite, in deep devotion, the bishop of London spoke. On behalf of the king, and for himself, he made his confession.

5966 'My lords', said the bishop, 'listen to me now. You see our lord the king here present; he has come to the martyr in faith and in love; he orders me to declare his unreserved confession for him, exactly as I and others have heard it in private. He declares before God and before the martyr that he did not have Saint Thomas killed or murdered, nor did he command that he should be struck at or killed, but he freely admits that he did use such words as were the cause and origin of his being murdered. And therefore, since he was, as he acknowledges, the cause of his death, he has come to the martyr, guilty and suppliant, he yields himself to him, admitting his guilt and wretchedness, he begs the saint to forgive his offence and he puts himself upon the judgment of you all to decide how he shall make atonement. He returns all her holdings to this holy church, both to the Archbishop and to the whole monastery, with the full liberty and dignity that she has in any place among Christian folk, and just as she used to have it in years gone by. The king now asks each and all of you to pray to the true martyr who now lies here, beseeching him to lay aside all anger and wrath, for he has done wrong towards him, he acknowledges his guilt, and he has come here to make atonement. And so that he may through your prayers and orisons, through true repentance and reparation, win the love of that most dear baron, he grants to this house land worth £10 yearly, in addition to the £30 worth that he gave you before.'

5996 When the bishop had finished speaking, King Henry confirmed all that he had said. The monastery remitted all anger against him; they granted him what he had begged for; and the prior kissed him on behalf of the whole house.

6001 Then King Henry humbled himself deeply, so deeply as to bring them all to tears: he himself took off his cloak, in the sight of them all, and thrust his head and shoulders into one of the openings of the tomb, leaving his back unprotected. He did not, however, take off his green tunic, so that I do not know if he was wearing a hair shirt, as he would not let this be seen. Then he had himself disciplined, first by the superiors, and then by over 80 monks. You would have seen almost all of them weeping tears of compassion. The bishop of London held the whip in his hand; he looked towards the holy body and then at the king:

6013 'Saint Thomas, true martyr', he said, 'hear me. If you are in such favour with God as it is said, and as I believe to be true, have mercy on this sinner here before me.' In faith and in love the saint listened to this man who had so often done him such great harm in this world, and who now prayed to him for himself and for another man. The martyr saw their hearts, his and the king's; and in true repentance they both found salvation. The king gave to Saint Thomas in reconciliation a good £40 worth of rents in perpetuity, and gold weighed out to make a shrine for him. Sincere penitence was dearer to him than Anjou, England, or France. The bishop of London struck the king five times, for the five senses in which he had sinned against God; then the bishop of Rochester beat him next; then the abbot of Boxley,[8] who was there; and then he received three blows from each of the monks.

6031 When King Henry had been flogged and punished and by atonement was reconciled to God, he withdrew his head and stood up; then he went and sat beside a pillar on the dirty ground, with no carpet or cushion under him, and sang psalms and prayers all night. He laid aside his anger against Saint Thomas's men; he asked forgiveness of Saint Thomas's sister and gave her a mill in reparation; she gets a good 10 marks rent a year from it.[9] He remained awake, praying, all the whole night, without getting up for any bodily need, until after matins. Then he got to his feet and went and adored God at all the altars; he came to the martyr fasting, having neither eaten nor drunk. At daybreak, he had mass sung. And he had his shoes put on again, all dirty and muddy as he was; no one could persuade him to let his feet be washed—it is impossible to hear tell of a more penitent prince! And yet he put off going to the martyr till it was almost too late. Sins are expiated by 40 day penances; the king was still delaying after 40 months. If he had waited a further 40 weeks, and then 40 more days, I can promise you that vengeance would have been exacted. And when the 40 months were gone by and the 40 weeks had begun, the whole of England was troubled. God's wrath would have been felt in one of these three periods, if Saint Thomas had not turned his face away.

Garnier Discusses Henry's Difficulties

6061 Now God has put away all his anger against the king. On the very day that he made his atonement, the Count of Flanders, who was attempting to destroy England, withdrew from the sea, with all his forces.[10] And on the following day the king of Scotland was captured.[11] Normandy had been almost entirely destroyed and made desolate, and the French army had got almost as far as Rouen; the whole of England was stirred up towards its own destruction—they had turned away from the heavens and were clinging to the clouds, but God the merciful had looked upon that unhappy people. They did not want to have such a powerful king over them but preferred to have a suckling child amongst them, one whom they could pull this way and that like a glove. Under this allegiance, they were doing harm everywhere, using the child as a cloak to hide their great treachery. The child could not govern the realm; no one could protect it more faithfully than his father. Father and son are one, if it be considered rightly, and those who try to separate father from son are trying to disinherit them both. But now I advise the king to allow holy church her rights and her liberties as he promised to do; to love his free men; to be moderate in justice, not taking vengeance for animals upon the bodies of men; to allow each man his rights; and to avoid covetousness. But I understand the king's heart and character–he has an insolent people to rule over. The slightest chance or excuse acts on them like a goad–give them the river bank to do what they like with, and they will not leave one sheep or pig on the heath. If the Normans were not afraid of him, if the English and Angevins, Bretons and Welsh, Scots and Poitevins did not all fear him, they would reduce the whole kingdom to want and misery in a moment.

6094 But whatever he may seem to be, he will make a good end. I heard Master Feramin[12] recounting a vision: before Saint Thomas was killed in the holy church, he saw a great procession going along beside the bell tower; he could see Saint Thomas riding on the left, with a clerk some way away from him whom he could not recognise. The king was on the other side, riding a great warhorse. There was a golden crown hanging from the cross, and the bearer held it up high as he went ahead of them. Then they heard a voice above them in the air, calling out that whoever should put jewels and bright gold upon the cross would have a golden crown in heaven eternally. They heard the voice clearly–Saint Thomas listened–now, if only he can, he will reach the cross! for he longed ardently for a heavenly crown. He was riding a big horse, and went in that direction; he placed many jewels and much fine gold upon the cross. After this, long after this, it occurred to the king that he would be disgraced if he did not reach it. His horse was good, he got to the cross, and put many pure gems on it, and tried gold, but it was not as much as the good priest had put. And then the clerk went along, trying to think how he could reach it; he did get there, riding hard, and put many jewels and much shining gold on it; he managed very well, but did not give nearly as much as the first of the two who had made offerings.

6121 The procession goes on, the world decays. Most people go there on foot, for no other place is so longed for. May Saint Thomas the martyr bring us real help! But I can tell you one thing for certain: the day will come when the king will give up all worldly glories for God.

No one knows what he clings to in his heart, but he is troubled by the instability of his kingdom, and by his children, little strengthened by good sense as they are. Then there are Merlin's prophecies;[13] these really alarmed him, and the fools who interpret them have been no help to him. For it was in Brittany that these foolish plans were worked out through which he was brought under restraint and all but brought to the ground. Look and see how much gold the hen eagle[14] had spread there; she has built nests oftener now than three times and three; the third nest, in England, made her heart glad.[15] She will rejoice, please God, in this one and in the others. But it will be a sad day if ever the king should mistrust this hen eagle; she will not build any nests anywhere else, she has lost her feathers and will hatch nothing more. But *[6140]* let the land be carefully guarded still, for this is very necessary. But the king ought to realise, and I tell him truly, that his sons will be fine men, strong and brave; and if they stand by each other, they will be all the stronger. Englishmen, Poitevins and Normans will go in fear of them; they will make some weep who are laughing at present. As long as father and son love each other, and they both love their daughter-in-law[16] and mother, as long as the children hold together like brothers and the king is over them as king and emperor—then whoever may mix the sauce, will find it very bitter himself. I pray to God and to the martyr whom I have served so many days, that he will bring peace to the kingdom and keep father and son, daughter-in-law and wife, in true amity, and give them joy and long life without change of lord—and that he will put it into their heads to do honour to me.

Conclusion

6156 Guernes the clerk of Le Pont here brings to an end his discourse on the martyr Saint Thomas and his passion. He has read it many a time by the baron's tomb, and has put nothing in it which is not true. May the merciful God grant him true forgiveness of all his sins.

No story as good as this has ever been composed; it was made and corrected at Canterbury and contains nothing but the exact truth. The verse consists of five-line stanzas rhymed together. And my language is good, for I was born in France. I began this account the second year after the saint was killed in his church, and I have worked hard at it; I learned the true facts from those who were close to Saint Thomas, and I have often taken out parts I had already written, in order to avoid inaccuracy. And in the fourth year I finished it. Let all those who shall hear this Life know that they will hear pure truth throughout; let all those who have written about the saint, in the romance tongue or in Latin, and who do not go this way, know that where they differ from me, they are wrong.

6176 Now let us pray to Jesus Christ, son of St. Mary, that for the love of Saint Thomas he may give us his help, so that nothing may be lacking to us in this bodily life, and that we may be so cleansed from the folly of this world, that when we die, we may have his company.

AMEN

Here ends the life of Saint Thomas the Martyr.

POSTSCRIPT

THE ABBESS, Saint Thomas's sister,[1] for her own honour and for the baron's sake, gave me a palfrey and its trappings; the very spurs were included. It was a fair throw of the dice that sent me to her house—and she does not do badly out of it either, for I shall repay her by singing her praises to everyone I meet, great and small. No one could find a better woman between here and Patras. Her ladies too, they made me positively fat, each giving me some gift—now may God ever lavish on them both bread and wine, meat and fish. And when their bodies lie silent and still, may God grant their souls true forgiveness.

Never again shall I cry 'Alas!', for I have been serving the kindest of lords. How tired I have got, putting his sufferings into verse, but he has repaid me splendidly, indeed he has; he finds me plentiful supplies, gold, silver, clothes in my bag, horses, and other things besides. If anyone says to me, 'Garnier, where are you going?'—all the world is mine! Why, I can say nothing but good of Judas (as long as he comes to confession).

Odo,[2] the good prior of Holy Trinity, and all the lords of the monastery have given me great help; may God be grateful to them! They have supplied me generously out of their own goods, they have put me up and supported me amongst themselves for a year and more. Whenever I may journey, up the world and down, my refuge is always with them because of their very great kindness; I have met nothing to surpass it anywhere in Christendom.

Explicit Vita sancti Thome archiepiscopi et martiris Canturiencis.

NOTES

Prologue

1. Thomas was canonised on 21 February 1173.

2. This refers to the 'criminous clerks' controversy: Henry's insistence that clerics accused of crimes should be subject to royal justice, which could kill, not merely to ecclesiastical tribunals, which could only imprison or unfrock.

3. The cathedral church at Canterbury.

4. i.e., a lady of religion, a nun. All the MSS have this word in the singular.

Chapter One

1. On 21 December, probably in 1118, perhaps as late as 1120. Becket is a Norman name. The site of his parents' house in Cheapside is known, as his sister later built the hospital of St. Thomas Acon there, which was subsequently replaced by the Mercers' Hall.

2. Genesis xxxvii, 9; Matthew xix, 28.

3. 'Coverlet' translates *palie*, a word which also suggests the idea of the *pallium*, the vestment symbolising papal authority conferred on each new archbishop.

4. Now a market, then open fields outside the city wall, some half a mile from Cheapside.

5. He was sent to the priory at Merton, in Surrey, for a time.

6. A Norman baron who was probably not much older than Thomas, since he appears as a member of Henry II's court and a signatory of the Constitutions of Clarendon some 30 years after this period. He died in 1176. It was at his castle at Pevensey that Thomas began to learn the ways of polite society.

7. Of Paris.

8. See J. H. Round, *Geoffrey de Mandeville*, pp. 374-5, and his *Commune of London*, pp. 113-124, for Osbern 'Octodenarii' or Eightpence, justiciar of London about 1139-42. FitzStephen says that Thomas was now clerk to the sheriffs and 'learned the wisdom of this world'. *Materials*, III, 14.

9. Theobald, of Norman knightly family, statesman and man of God; Archbishop of Canterbury 1138-1161.

10. This assertion contradicts without deigning expressly to notice the rumours put about by Thomas's enemies: that he was

introduced to Theobald's household in a shabby condition, with no proper attendance, the mere hanger-on of some menial.

11. One of Thomas's most ardent opponents. Became archdeacon of Canterbury, 1147; Archbishop of York, 1154; died 1181. See Knowles, *Episcopal Colleagues of Thomas Becket*, pp. 12-14 and generally.

12. Garnier's phrase, *le clerc Baille-Hache*, can be understood as I have taken it, but this may be wrong. It could mean that Roger called Thomas 'Baille-Hache the clerk', which would fit in better with Grim's version ('the clerk with an axe'—*clericum cum ascia. Materials*, II, 362), but not so well with Garnier's own context. *Bailler* = to give, take, or carry; *hache* = an axe.

13. William FitzHerbert, died Whitsun 1154, canonised 1227.

14. The collegiate church of St. John of Beverley, Yorkshire. He held this appointment from 1139 to 1154.

15. Theobald is thought to have done this deliberately for the sake of the church, which, with the advent of so strong a monarch as Henry seemed likely to be, would be in danger of losing some of the independence it had gained during the Anarchy. He may even have intended that Thomas should succeed him at Canterbury.

16. Henry was crowned on 19 December 1154; the earliest extant charters witnessed by Thomas as Chancellor date from January 1155. Knowles points out that the chancellorship was not a major office until Thomas himself by his success in it made it so. *Archbishop Thomas Becket*, Raleigh Lecture 1949, p. 9.

17. I cannot identify Vivian. William of Canterbury speaks of 'a townsman', *oppidanus. Materials*, I, 6.

18. FitzStephen says that Thomas's troops and the trumpets peculiar to them were well known on both sides of the fighting. *Materials*, III, 35.

19. Born 1155, crowned 1170, died 1183.

20. The authenticity of this passage, from 'Has he behaved . . .', is doubtful; it occurs in only one of the MSS and is not supported by any of the Latin *Lives*, one of which says just the opposite. *Materials*, III, 26.

21. Louis VII, 1137-1180.

22. They were: Bartholomew, bishop of Exeter 1161, died 1184; Hilary, bishop of Chichester 1147, died 1169; and Walter (brother of Theobald), bishop of Rochester 1148, died 1182.

23. Chief justiciar of England; died 1179.

24. The chapter of Canterbury cathedral consisted of the monks of the Benedictine abbey of Holy Trinity. The Archbishop was also their abbot.

25. Prior Wibert, 1150-1167.

26. This means Gilbert Foliot, at that time still bishop of Hereford; translated to London almost a year after the meeting now being discussed, in April 1163.

27. Henry of Blois, brother of King Stephen; bishop of Winchester 1129; elected to Canterbury 1136 but prevented by St. Bernard from taking up the post; consoled with legatine powers which enabled him to make Theobald's episcopacy difficult. Died 1171.

28. No other text mentions this.

29. Thomas was ordained priest 2 June 1162 and consecrated next day, Trinity Sunday.

30. The Benedictine habit was black; a novice making his solemn profession was formally robed in it to signify his withdrawal from the world.

31. Some of the MSS say 'Alnwick'.

32. Appointed Archbishop of Canterbury 1052, but recognised only by a schismatic Pope; deposed 1070; died in prison at Winchester, 1072.

33. Appointed to the see of Canterbury, 958; died in the Alps on his journey to fetch the pallium. 'Mount Jove' was the old name for the Great St. Bernard.

34. A former monk of Cluny; prior of Bermondsey, 1157; abbot of Evesham, 1161; died 1191. *D.N.B.*

35. The vestment granted by the Pope to the archbishop as a symbol of the latter's papal authority.

36. The other members of the embassy were: John, treasurer of York, later bishop of Poitiers; John of Salisbury; Jordan of Chichester; Simon, a monk of Canterbury.

37. Alexander III, 1159-1181.

Chapter Two

1. Thomas's secretary.

2. This was not an unreasonable idea; the two posts were held together both before and after Thomas's time.

3. A royal palace near Oxford.

4. The sheriff's aid was in fact a variable rate, assessed locally; it was the Danegeld that was two shillings on the hide. Round, *Feudal England*, p. 501.

5. Garnier is anticipating; the council of Westminster, 1 October 1163, was the result of this and similar cases.

6. Philip de Broi had been tried for murder and acquitted by the bishop of Lincoln's court; Simon FitzPeter, said to be his personal enemy, was sheriff of Bedfordshire and justice in eyre in the same county, and insisted on re-opening the case.

7. Garnier has misinterpreted his source. Grim, taken with William of Canterbury (*Materials*, II, 375, and I, 13), shows that Philip was to provide rods with which he would be beaten; hence the need to strip. Grim calls these rods, *arma,* and Garnier has thought that the reference was to the practice of offering an oath upon arms.

8. This is the council of Westminster, 1 October 1163.

9. That is, they offered him only a qualified obedience reserving the right to disobey him if loyalty to the church should demand it.

10. Henry I, 1100-1135.

11. Arnulf, bishop of Lisieux 1141-1174; died 1184; 'a consummate diplomatist . . . with whose services no party could afford to dispense.' Norgate, *England under the Angevin Kings,* I, p. 500.

12. Robert de Chesney, Foliot's uncle; bishop of Lincoln 1148; died 1166. 'Not a man of strong character'—Knowles, *E.C.*, p. 16.

13. Some of the MSS have 'Gloucester'.

14. A manor near Faversham, Kent, belonging to the see of Canterbury.

15. Born in England, probably before 1100; a pupil of Hugh of St. Victor and of Abelard; taught in Paris and at Melun, his pupils including John of Salisbury, Thomas Becket, Roger of Worcester. Bishop of Hereford 1163; died 1167.

16. John I, Count of Vendôme, 1136-1192.

17. Prior of Clairvaux under St. Bernard; abbot of the daughter house of l'Aumône 1156-1171.

18. Clarendon palace, near Salisbury, Wiltshire. This meeting took place in January 1164.

19. Jocelin de Bohun, bishop of Salisbury 1142; suspended by Thomas 1166, for giving way to royal pressure and making the excommunicate John of Oxford his dean; excommunicated 1169 and 1170; died 1184.

20. William Turbe, bishop of Norwich 1146; a man of learning and courage, respected by Thomas. Died 1174.

21. Robert de Beaumont 1104-1168: chief justiciar jointly with Richard de Lucy 1155-1168.

22. Reginald, a natural son of Henry I, thus uncle to the present king. Died 1175.

23. Richard of Hastings was Master of the Temple in England from 1155 till 1176 certainly, 1185 probably. Osto of St. Omer, also called Hosteus de Bolonia (Boulogne), was another well-known

Templar. B. A. Lees cites them both as being prominent among those 'courtier knights' who were 'active political instruments of Henry II, of special value in the tangled foreign relations of the Angevin dynasty'. Beatrice A. Lees, *Records of the Templars*, pp. xlviii-liv.

24. This does not adequately translate the original *sur defens del clergie,* which I do not understand. Walberg suggests that Garnier has misread his source.

25. The Pope's letter absolving Thomas is dated from Sens, 1 April (1164).

26. Rotrou de Beaumont, son of Henry de Newburgh, Earl of Warwick; bishop of Evreux 1140; archbishop of Rouen 1165; died 1183.

27. On Portsmouth harbour, Hampshire.

28. A clerk of the royal chapel; at Henry's insistence, the bishop of Salisbury made him his dean in 1166, as a reward for work done on an embassy to the antipope, but the appointment was quashed and he himself excommunicated because he had taken an oath to the antipope; and because some members of Salisbury chapter were in exile with Thomas, so that the Pope had prohibited the election; he was soon absolved and re-established; became bishop of Norwich 1175; died 1200.

29. A clerk in the service of Thomas when he was chancellor; became archdeacon of Canterbury 1163, or 'archdevil' as Thomas put it; excommunicated by Thomas, May 1169; absolved by the Pope the same year; elected bishop of Ely 1173; consecrated in 1174, after clearing himself by oath of complicity in Thomas's death, and of having been married while in holy orders. Seems to have had custody of the royal seal from 1166, though without the title of chancellor. Died 1189.

30. For the archbishop of York, not personally.

31. I Kings I and II.

32. Apocrypha, I Maccabees II, 48, 'neither gave they a horn to the sinner'; Revised Version: neither suffered they the sinner to triumph'.

33. Much legend surrounds both Simon Magus (Acts VIII, 9-13) and Nero, emperor of Rome 54-68 A.D. Simon is supposed to have visited Rome and performed various magical feats; Nero, it was thought, was not dead and would return. Garnier must mean that if Nero did come back he would find the original Simonist well established among the bishops.

34. Exodus IV, 14. The point is that Aaron spoke on behalf of Moses, which is what the bishops are not doing on behalf of Thomas.

35. Late Latin writer whose Fables were a popular schoolbook.

36. New Romney, Kent, one of the Cinque Ports.

37. Occupant of the manor of Charing, near Canterbury, and possessed of other lands in Kent; probably a lawyer; was one of a board appointed to administer the property of the see after Henry had appropriated it; named in 1169 as one whom Thomas would excommunicate if he did not repent; later founded a leper hospital at Romney in honour of St. Stephen and St. Thomas of Canterbury. William Urry, 'Two notes on Guernes de Pont Sainte-Maxence', *Archaeologia Cantiana* lxvi 92-95; and *Canterbury under the Angevin Kings*, pp. 180-1.

Chapter Three

1. The Northampton council was summoned for Tuesday, 6 October 1164; business began on the 8th, Thursday.

2. Henry had offered him the insult of not summoning him directly, as the great barons were normally summoned, but merely instructing the sheriff of Kent to order him to be present.

3. The barons' later objection to this encroachment of royal over seigneurial justice is embodied in clause 34 of Magna Carta.

4. Son of Gilbert, hereditary marshal of Henry I.

5. He claimed Mundham, part of the archiepiscopal manor of Pagham, Sussex.

6. Essoins; formal legal excuses.

7. Versicles sung at mass on certain festivals.

8. Perhaps Walter and Gilbert. Four other sons survived him, one being William, later Earl Marshal, regent of England 1216-1219.

9. See Knowles, *E.C.* appendix V, for a discussion of Thomas's illness.

10. The biographers differ about this.

11. Roger, a younger son of Robert, earl of Gloucester, and so a cousin of Henry II; consecrated bishop of Worcester in 1164, by Thomas, who often reminded him of this link between them, 'The most loyal . . . perhaps also the most spiritual of Thomas's colleagues.' Knowles, *E.C.* p. 22. Died 1179.

12. *N'est trop buens a porter la cruiz que vus veez. Veez* may mean 'see' or 'forbid'; *que* may be a relative pronoun referring to *la cruiz* or to the subject of *est*; or it may mean 'because'. The Latin source reads *Non est enim nimis bonus qui portet crucem Domini sui. Materials,* IV, 47.

13. This and subsequent repetitions may be due to interpolation of material by scribes; or to lack of final polishing by the author; or it may be an attempt to build up tension in the audience, in the style of epics.

14. See the previous note.

15. The bishops had by now withdrawn, so as not to sentence their superior.

16. The king's brother, a natural son of Geoffrey of Anjou; became Earl of Warren and of Surrey 1164; said to have had the sight of an eye restored to him by St. Thomas (*Materials*, I, 452); died 1202.

17. Hugh Wake or Wac, lord of Bourne in right of his wife.

18. He was at odds with Thomas already, because he held the fief of Saltwood from the crown, which Thomas was claiming for the archbishopric; see p. 120 and n. Later he was put in charge of the property of the see of Canterbury; and employed to drive Thomas's relatives and dependants into exile; Thomas excommunicated him several times. The murderers in 1170 used Saltwood as their base.

19. Some of the biographers say that Thomas riposted sharply.

20. Walberg identifies this man with the *Petrus de Mortorio* mentioned by Anonymous I as Thomas's squire. *Materials*, IV, 52.

21. Two canons of the priory of Sempringham in Lincolnshire; see below. Scaiman occurs again in the story; *Materials*, IV, 57 and VI, 77.

22. *Quemdam famulum suum proprium nomine Rogerium de Brai, strenuum valde et fidelem*; *Materials*, IV, 53.

23. The mother house of the Gilbertine order.

24. It was also very near St. Andrew's monastery where he was staying.

25. The third hour, ending at 9 a.m.

26. In later years he became keeper of the back gate of the monastery at Canterbury, and was allowed 'the corrody of one monk' in honour of St. Thomas, on the understanding that future gate-keepers were not to expect this concession. Urry, *Canterbury under the Angevin Kings*, p. 183.

27. *Mais la premiere nuit qu'il s'en fu si emblez / Le secunt jur, tut dreit est en Nicole entrez.* Grim says the party journeyed all night and reached Lincoln as dawn was breaking (*Materials*, II, 399); Herbert of Bosham has them stopping for a night at 'Graham' (Grantham, Greetham, or Gretton). It is 79 miles from Northampton to Lincoln.

28. Jacob or James, a fuller; seems to have lived just above the bridge over the Witham.

29. An isolated retreat in the fens, possibly where Hermitage Farm now stands near to what was a loop of the Witham, since straightened. I am indebted to the on-the-spot researches of Dr. Urry for this suggestion.

Chapter Four

1. They went on to Boston, where presumably they tried but failed to get a boat; then upriver again to Haverholme, a Gilbertine

priory; then south to Chicksand Priory in Bedfordshire; and are next heard of in Kent, at Eastry near the port of Sandwich.

2. On the open shore, not at a port, east of Calais. He was now in the territory of Matthew, Count of Boulogne, who might be expected to be hostile, both as a cousin of King Henry's, and for Thomas's opposition to his marriage in 1160 to the abbess of Romsey, Stephen's daughter, heiress of the county of Boulogne.

3. To the Cistercian abbey of St. Bertin, near St. Omer.

4. Santiago de Compostella in north-east Spain.

5. Homage was a mutual obligation, binding the lord as much as the vassal, and could be renounced by either party. Liege homage to the overlord always overrode all lesser homages, so that no doubt Richard felt free to continue to hold his fiefs, which in any case all derived ultimately from the king, while renouncing any obligation to Thomas See *E.H.D.* II, 938, for extracts from Glanville bearing on this point.

6. Philippe d'Alsace, brother of the Count of Boulogne, now ruling Flanders for his father who was away in the Holy Land.

7. The adjective used is *riches*; this meant 'powerful' almost more than it meant 'wealthy'.

8. Milo, of English birth; succeeded his uncle as bishop of Thérouanne, 1159; died 1169.

9. A monk of Clairvaux; made cardinal by Eugenius III.

10. A relative of Foliot's; baron of the Exchequer; justice in eyre; bishop of Winchester 1174; died 1188.

11. William of Aubigny, Earl of Arundel in right of his wife Adeliza, widow of Henry I; died 1176.

12. In Latin, *Franco*. Louis sent for *fratem Franconem, domini papae camerarium. Materials*, IV, 60; V, 117.

13. Thomas was no longer an almost solitary fugitive; he was escorted by 300 men provided by Louis, and had been joined at Clairmarais by Herbert of Bosham and others from Canterbury.

14. A baron of the Exchequer, justice in eyre, dean of Waltham.

15. Later sheriff of Hants., Northants. and Devon; one of the governors of the Young King; justice in eyre.

16. One of the signatories of the Constitutions of Clarendon; and see Walberg, p. 256.

17. Baron of the Exchequer, justice in eyre, royal chamberlain; held lands in Wiltshire; died 1177 or 1178.

18. This was Hilary of Chichester.

19. Gilbert Foliot.

20. This was Reginald FitzJocelin, son of the bishop of Salisbury, also called 'the Lombard'. He was archdeacon of Salisbury, became bishop of Bath, aged 23, in 1174; elected archbishop of Canterbury 1191, but died almost immediately. Herbert lists him

among Thomas's *eruditi.* See Knowles, *E.C.*, p. 112, for his 'ambiguous behaviour' at this time.

21. This translates not the text, but Walberg's emendation of it. The French reads: *E quant ne porent faire* . . . 'since they could not do . . .'

22. A former monk of Clairvaux; archdeacon of Pavia; cardinal; bishop of Porto, 1176; died 1177.

23. The Constitutions of Clarendon will be found in Latin in Walberg, pp. 259 ff, and in Stubbs's *Charters*, pp. 163-167; and in English in *E.H.D.* II, 718 ff.

24. 'Advocate' translates *avoez*—the lay patron, the protector, and usually the man with the right of presentation to the living.

25. i.e., they might be bound upon oath to correct the fault for which they were excommunicated, but not made to bind themselves more generally.

26. *Ipse erit in misericordia domini regis.*

27. i.e., those under sentence of forfeiture were not to try to protect their movables from the royal officers by storing them on church premises.

28. Garnier has managed to find objections to nearly all the Constitutions, but the Pope did not condemn so many. Neither he nor Thomas objected to this one.

29. A Cistercian monastery not far from Sens, but outside Louis' territory, as it was in Burgundy. Guichard was its second abbot (1136-1165).

30. Roger, bishop of Worcester.

31. These men were both made sheriffs in 1170, Walter, of Lincolnshire, and Wimer, of Norfolk and Suffolk. Walberg, p. 264, identifies Wimer with Wimarus, a former clerk of Hugh, earl of Norfolk, whom Thomas excommunicated in 1169.

32. Hugh Bigod, earl of Norfolk; the Pope excommunicated him in 1166 for allegedly depriving the Augustinian canons of Pentney, near King's Lynn, of some of their lands; then absolved him conditionally in 1167, with a suspended sentence to fall one year later if he did not reform. This brings the edict of Henry's quoted here to 1168 or 1169. The story is complicated: see Knowles *E.C.*, pp. 127-8.

33. Cnut was king of England 1016-1035. Peter's Pence is thought to date from a tribute first paid to Rome by Offa, king of the Mercians, in 787. It lapsed later, and was revived by William I.

34. The Young King was not crowned till June 1170. Garnier is following Grim, who misplaces this event.

35. Matthew, V, 13, 14.

36. Isaiah LVI, 10.

37. Proverbs XI, 22--'As a jewel of gold in a swine's snout, so is a fair woman which is without discretion'.

Chapter Five

1. The following letter was written in the first half of 1166; see *Materials*, V, 266. Garnier's versions of these documents are not exact —sometimes he makes a précis, sometimes he omits or adds a phrase or two, occasionally he misinterprets. He leaves out all references to classical authors and often introduces extra biblical comparisons.

2. Constantine the Great, Roman Emperor, died 337.

3. Garnier's phrasing does not make sense here; he seems to have misunderstood his original. See *Materials*, V, 271, or the same quoted in Walberg, p. 267.

4. This translates *despensatur*, which in turn stands for *dispensatores*; these words also meant 'stewards' but the main reference is to the role of the priest in distributing the sacrament.

5. i.e., who has the right to administer (spiritual) punishment.

6. Luke, X, 16.

7. II Chronicles, XXVI.

8. II Kings, XVI.

9. II Samuel, VI, 3-7.

10. *Materials*, V, 275, note b: 'this statement is fabulous'.

11. Innocent I, 402-417; St. John Chrysostome, *c.* 347-407, patriarch of Constantinople.

12. St. Ambrose, *c.* 339-397, bishop of Milan, excommunicated Theodosius the Great, Roman Emperor 379-395, for a massacre at Thessalonica in 390.

13. Henry had convoked a conference at Chinon, in Touraine, in May 1166, to prepare for his invasion of Brittany, and to deal with the problem raised by the Pope's having made Thomas legate of England, except for the province of York.

14. See *Materials*, V, 278 ff for the text of this letter.

15. Garnier's text is confused. His original reads: *non habetis . . . interdicere episcopis ne tractent causas de transgressione fidei vel juramenti, et multa in hunc modum, quae scripta sunt inter consuetudines vestras, quas dicitis avitas. Materials*, V. 281.

16. Leviticus, XVIII, 5 and Isaiah, X, 1-2.

17. In the schism which developed after the death of Adrian IV in 1159, the English and French kings recognised Alexander III, while the Emperor Frederick Barbarossa supported the antipope Victor IV. In May 1165 Henry had sent an embassy to Wurzburg, which had given some kind of undertaking that Henry would abjure Alexander III and support the antipope Paschal.

18. *Materials*, V, 408; Morey and Brooke, *Letters of Gilbert Foliot*, pp. 222-225.

19. Garnier misrepresents his source, which speaks of its better being to be praised for bearing poverty rather than known to all for ingratitude. Walberg, p. 270.

20. Matilda the Empress, 1102-1167.

21. See page 29, n. 28, for Thomas's excommunication of John of Oxford.

22. *Materials*, V, 512 ff.

23. II Corinthians, I, 17.

24. Luke, X, 19.

25. Ezekiel, II, 6: 'Be not afraid of them . . . though briers and thorns be with thee, and thou dost dwell among scorpions'.

26. The idea of obedience is not in the original; Garnier brings it in. One would have expected Thomas to consider Foliot altogether too obedient to Henry—perhaps Garnier is thinking of the bishop's duty of obedience to the king's truest needs.

27. I Corinthians, XII, 23.

28. The fifth commandment; Exodus, XX, 12.

29. Garnier's text appears to contradict itself here, saying in effect 'you are doing this secretly, you are doing it openly'. I have tried to resolve the contradiction by the use of punctuation marks. The original reads; *sed (quod deterius est) cum persecutoribus meis, et in me Dei et ecclesiae ipsius, et boc non in occulto, stare non erubescis. Materials*, V, 517-8.

30. Deuteronomy, XXXII, 42.

31. *Tunicae meae timeo—Materials*, V, 518. Perhaps some proverb?

32. Psalm 82.

33. Exodus, VII, 1—'And the Lord said unto Moses, See, I have made thee a god to Pharaoh.'

34. Exodus, XXII, 28.

35. Garnier has misunderstood his original, which reads: *Et de eo qui juraturus erat, loquens per Moysen, ait, 'Applica illum ad Deos,' id est ad sacerdotes; Materials*, V, 519; the reference is to Exodus, XXII, 8-11, in which anyone suspected of theft is to clear himself by oath.

36. Malachi, II, 7.

37. I Corinthians, VI, 3.

38. Deuteronomy, XVII, 12.

39. 'Equally' translates *par igal guise*, possibly just a line filler, or perhaps a misunderstanding of the original, which read: *vos commonefacio, rogo et obsecro* (*Materials*, V, 520). *Commonefacere* = to remind forcibly, to impress upon.

40. William Rufus, 1087-1100; and Henry I, 1100-1135.

Chapter Six

1. From November, 1164, to the same month 1166.

2. The Cistercians were skilled water engineers; see Knowles, *Historian and Character*, pp. 198 ff.

3. No doubt he was also moved by the excommunications Thomas had pronounced at Vézelay, 12 July 1166.

4. Cîteaux, mother house of the Cistercian order, is in Burgundy, some 16 miles south of Dijon. The meetings were annual. The present abbot was Gilbert 'the Theologian', 1163-67, English by birth.

5. Garin de Galardun succeeded Guichard at Pontigny; became archbishop of Bourges, 1174; died 1180.

6. Only Grim and Garnier say that Louis went himself to Pontigny; Herbert of Bosham tells how Thomas sent him to Louis, and how Louis commissioned him to invite Thomas to come to him. *Materials*, III, 402-3.

7. A Benedictine abbey near Sens.

8. From November 1166 to November 1170.

9. Garnier's chronology is at fault, as the Young King's homage to Louis, in January 1169, and the meeting at St. Leger did not take place until after the events he discusses on pp. 102-111.

10. This is near Rambouillet in the Ile-de-France. The date was 7 February 1169. The evidence for the several meetings of the two kings, or their representatives, over this six-year period is worked out by Louis Halphen in 'Les entrevues des rois Louis VII et Henri II durant l'exil de Thomas Becket en France', in *Melanges d'histoire offerts a M. Charles Bemont* (Paris, 1913), pp. 151-162. He establishes the dates and locations of 10 such meetings and of two that were planned but did not take place. Garnier's version is far from correct. See also Walberg, pp. lxxxiv ff.

11. A conference was planned for January 1170, in Tours, but it did not take place.

12. Perhaps this refers to Hilary's abashed silence when his Latin caused such amusement to the Curia in November 1164 at Sens.

13. His chaplain, Robert of Merton; his servant, Brun, who washed his hair clothes; but who was the third?

14. A canon of the same priory in Surrey where Thomas had been to school as a child, but not to be confused, as he often has been, with the Robert who was its prior and died in 1150, or with his successor, also called Robert, who died in 1167.

Chapter Seven

1. In April 1165.

2. No other source mentions Nogent-le-Rotrou. Halphen tentatively identifies this meeting with one said by Robert de Torigni to have taken place at about Easter 1166.

3. This is probably the meeting which took place not at Montmirail but at Les Planches, near Gisors in the Vexin, in November 1167.

4. An error: William of Pavia was one of the cardinals present, but the other was Otto of St. Nicholas.

5. Chartres is 40 miles from Montmirail, about 70 from Les Planches.

6. Henry was not present at the Les Planches conference; the Pope's messengers went to him at Caen.

7. Montmirail is near La Ferté-Bernard; it, Nogent-le-Rotrou and Fréteval are all in the area where the borders of Normandy, Maine and the county of Blois touch. This meeting, the chief aim of which was to arrange an end to the warfare between Louis and Henry, took place on 6 and 7 January 1169. There was another meeting a month later at St.-Léger-en-Yvelines; Garnier confuses the events of the two meetings.

8. Or de Corileto, former prior of the monastery of Grandmont, in Normandy.

9. By name, Simon. He and Bernard de la Coudre had been commissioned by the Pope in May 1168 to reconcile Henry and Thomas.

10. Archbishops of Canterbury 1070-89 and 1093-1109 respectively.

11. There is no other mention of this. John of Salisbury says that Henry proposed at St. Léger to ask the advice of the bishops of England. *Materials*, VI, 512.

12. No one else mentions Geoffrey Ridel in this context.

13. John Belmeis, originally from Canterbury, one of the young men of Theobald's court along with Thomas, Roger of Pont l'Evêque, and the rest. Became bishop of Poitiers, 1162; archbishop of Lyons, 1182-93; died *c.* 1200. See *Materials*, VI, 491, 493 and 511, for the present affair.

14. A place of pilgrimage just outside Paris.

15. Montmartre is between Paris and St. Denis. This conference took place in November 1169.

16. This translates *finé*, which may mean 'concluded', or 'broken off'. The Hippeau edition however reads *fixé*, 'arranged'.

17. Henry did say something not unlike this (*Materials*, VII, 164), but no other author suggests that clerks were actually sent for.

18. Between the districts of Touraine and Beauce, in July 1170. Garnier is just glancing ahead for a moment; we come back at once to the events that followed the Montmirail meeting.

19. Herbert of Bosham lists Gunther of Winchester among Thomas's *eruditi* as 'homo simplex et rectus, timoratus et sine querela', adding that what he lacked in 'scientia' he more than made up in 'vita'. *Materials*, III, 527.

20. See *Materials*, VII, 177.

21. Madoc does not seem to be otherwise recorded.

22. See *Materials*, VII, 204 ff.

23. It was Rotrou, archbishop of Rouen, whom the Pope sent, in commission with the bishop of Nevers and others. William of Sens (son of the Count of Champagne and Blois, twice regent of France) was however actively concerned in trying to reach a settlement, and was present at the Fréteval meeting.

24. Bernard of Saint-Sauge, became bishop of Nevers 1159, died 1176.

25. The conference at Fréteval, July 1170. Its chief purpose was political. *Materials*, VII, 338 ff.

26. Received the castle of Rhuddlan in Wales from Henry, 1157; baron of the Exchequer, 1168; remained loyal during the 1173-4 rebellion, defending Verneuil against Louis; killed in the Holy Land, 1187.

27. Herbert of Bosham, an eyewitness, though writing long after the event, says that Thomas invited himself to a meeting in Tours between Henry and Count Theobald of Blois. *Materials*, III, 468.

28. This passage may mean that Henry did not pay what he had promised to Thomas, or that Thomas (not having received this) could not pay his debts. FitzStephen says that Thomas had brought his creditors with him in the expectation of being able to settle up with them. *Materials*, III, 116. Eventually Rotrou lent him some money.

29. Or at Chaumont-sur-Loire; see Walberg, p. 286.

30. A *Ricardus Malban' miles Templi* is recorded in 1147; he or a similarly named man appears to have held high office among the Templars in England in 1155; the Malbanks were Palatine barons of Cheshire; the name is also found in Herefordshire, Essex, Herts., Beds., and Normandy. B. A. Lees, *Records of the Templars*, pp. li and 244.

31. Hugh may be the same clerk who took the letter from Henry to Thomas telling him to go to England at once. *Materials*, III, 114.

32. *Materials*, VII, 347.

33. An archiepiscopal fief and castle in a strategically important situation east of Romney Marsh, at the south end of Stone Street, the Roman road from the coast to Canterbury, near the port of Hythe. Its holder had been convicted of treason in 1163, and Henry had chosen to regard the fief as reverting to the crown, and had granted it to Ranulf de Broc. Thomas had claimed it, as well as other fiefs, as soon as he became Archbishop.

34. 22 July-11 November.

Chapter Eight

1. The great scholar; a member of Thomas's staff, as he had been of Theobald's. He had been in exile at Rheims, on his own account as well as on Thomas's. Arrived in England, 9 November.

2. *Materials*, VII, 400.

3. Thomas might reasonably have felt insulted that one of his principal enemies should have been appointed as his escort; but it proved a safeguard later. See below.

4. Roger, archbishop of York; Gilbert Foliot, of London; Jocelin, of Salisbury.

5. A brother of the Earl de Warenne who had died in the crusades; a signatory of the Constitutions of Clarendon; baron of the Exchequer; justice in eyre; sheriff of Sussex, 1170-76. His family had a particular antipathy towards Thomas because he had prevented the marriage of one of its daughters to the king's brother William.

6. Justiciar of London under Stephen; sheriff of London, then of Surrey and Kent jointly; justice in eyre; a 'great city magnate' who acquired land by lending money and foreclosing; Round, *Geoffrey de Mandeville*, p. 304.

7. In the Pas-de-Calais.

8. Boulogne was not at this time a cathedral town; Milo will have been the dean of a collegiate church.

9. Brother of Philip of Flanders; see above, p. 57, n. 6.

10. I have translated what Garnier said, but his version of his source is not correct. It reads: *nihil est enim quod magis hominibus debeatur quam ut suprema voluntas, postquam aliud velle non possunt, adimpleatur. Materials*, I, 86.

11. York, London and Salisbury were waiting for a wind to take them across the Channel to Henry, to discuss the filling of the vacant sees mentioned below. *Materials*, IV, 123.

12. He was treasurer of Canterbury cathedral. Probably he had done no more than put out to sea, and then had to put back again; he was not in exile with Thomas and is known to have been in England in October 1170.

13. See *Materials*, VII, 404, for Thomas's description of this episode. FitzStephen says that the king's officials demanded that any foreigners accompanying the Archbishop should either produce a letter from the king, or take an oath to him; 'a certain archdeacon of Sens' was the only one to whom this might apply, and he, Thomas told the officials, was travelling as part of his household and was therefore exempt from any such request. Simon must have been a man of substance; he had been particularly generous to Thomas and his exiled household. *Materials*, III, 119.

14. Prior to the monastery of St. Martin at Dover; formerly chaplain of Theobald; succeeded Thomas as archbishop of Canterbury; died 1184.

15. Several chroniclers say 'Woodstock', but Round has shown that it was indeed Winchester. *Feudal England*, pp. 506-7.

16. Geoffrey Ridel.

17. The six deceased bishops were: Hilary of Chichester; died 1169; Nigel of Ely, died 1169; Robert of Hereford, died 1167; Robert of Lincoln, died 1166; Robert of Bath and Wells, died 1166; Athelwolf of Carlisle, died 1156 or 1157.

18. The bishop of Ely, as we have just seen, was dead. Garnier has taken the word *Helmaniensis*, meaning the Bishop of Norwich, whose residence was at Elmham, to be a variant of *(H)eliensis*. See *Materials*, I, 106, and Walberg, p. xli.

19. These phrases echo what Grim says that Thomas said to the earls of Cornwall and Leicester at Northampton; *Materials*, II, 398. 'Leader' translates *chief*, literally 'head'; 'does so' translates *fait*, the reference being to beating.

20. On the same occasion at Northampton Thomas went on to compare priestly power to gold, royal to lead.

21. One of Henry's Norman vassals.

22. Jocelin of Louvain or of Arundel, brother of Henry I's second wife, Adeliza.

23. There were two interviews, not one. At the first, on 2 December at Canterbury, Thomas was ordered to recall his sentences of excommunication; the second was at Southwark on 18 December.

24. Garnier should have said the bishop of Winchester, not Worcester. The whole stanza is obscure and does not represent the Latin text clearly. See *Materials*, VII, 405, or the same in Walberg, p. 293.

25. This was uncommonly humble; prelates often confirmed from horseback.

26. This may allude to the candles miraculously relit at Newington (*Materials*, I, 310), or to the lights that the pilgrims' offerings kept burning at Thomas's shrine.

Chapter Nine

1. Nephew of Ranulf de Broc; originally a clerk, then a monk, who came back into the world, according to FitzStephen (*Materials*, III, 126); *thalami regii ostiarius* according to Benedict of Peterborough (*Materials*, II, 128); justice in eyre, 1185 and 1187. He had not personally cut off the horse's tail; it was his nephew John who did that, not, incidentally, in Thomas's presence. Robert was now in immediate charge of the archiepiscopal property which Henry had sequestered and which was being administered by Ranulf de Broc.

2. The archbishop of York was only suspended. Foliot and Jocelin were excommunicated.

2. I am not happy with this translation. The French reads: *vostre religiuns ne vus face turner*; Walberg suggests that a better reading might be *religiun*, thus making this word the object of the verb, not the subject. The meaning would then be something like 'lest he (Thomas) should affect your religious profession'.

4. Bur was a royal residence near Noron, south west of Bayeux in Normandy. The 'three companions' are the bishops; it is not clear whether Garnier is telling of their arrival twice, in epic style, or whether the bishops first sent the brief of excommunication in to King Henry and then later went to see him themselves.

5. An exaggeration; only Foliot and Jocelin were excommunicated, the rest were suspended.

6. When Harold was compelled to swear that he would help William of Normandy to gain the throne of England, he also promised to marry one of the duke's daughters. She is said to have died young, and her name is not known for certain.

7. i.e., the army which was to go and conquer England.

8. Possibly the archbishop of York, more likely the devil.

9. Winchelsea is of course in England, one of the Cinque Ports.

10. Hugh de Morville: a considerable landowner in the north of England; justice in eyre in Cumberland and Northumberland, 1170; signatory of the Constitutions of Clarendon; is probably, but not certainly, the same man who paid 15 marks and three horses for the right to hold court in 1200, and died in 1204. *D.N.B.*

William de Tracy: belonged to a family that held land in Devon and the south-west; died of an agonising illness in Sicily on his way to the Holy Land (*Materials*, III, 536-7), having granted the manor of Doccombe, Devon, to the chapter of Canterbury 'for love of the blessed Thomas'. *D.N.B.*

Reginald FitzUrse: held lands in chief of the king in Somerset, Kent and Northants.; his mother was a great-niece of Henry I. *D.N.B.*

Richard le Breton or Brito: less is known about him than the others, his surname being very common. Held lands in Somerset.

The later fate of these men is surrounded by legend. They fled to Scotland after the murder, but then came south again to de Morville's castle of Knaresborough, Yorkshire. They were excommunicated, but not pursued by lay justice. They are said to have been ordered by the Pope to take the cross, and to have died in the Holy Land.

11. The other biographers do make this accusation, but the archbishop of Sens writing to the Pope declared that 'the archdevil of York' and the 'apostates of London and Salisbury' did in real

truth—*veritate*—kill Thomas. Knowles says it was Roger of York's 'vindictive bitterness' that produced Henry's fit of fatal rage. *E.C.*, p. 139.

12. 29 December.

13. 'Reeve' translates *provoz*, meaning the *praepositus*. There was no mayor in Canterbury till much later. The reeve had both police and military duties, and collected tolls and royal rents; he was probably a crown official. This reeve may have been the John son of Vivian who held that post soon after Thomas's murder. Urry, *Canterbury under the Angevin Kings*, pp. 65 and 84-6.

14. Other narratives say that the servants were still at table.

15. William FitzNigel or FitzNeal. For his later life and his siege of the monastery in 1188, see Urry, *op. cit.*, p. 166.

16. Garnier has altered his source: Grim says that the knights at this point ordered Thomas to leave the kingdom (*Materials*, II, 432), to which the reply Thomas gives in Garnier's text is perfectly appropriate. The order to stay where he was came at the end of the interview.

17. On Christmas day Thomas had excommunicated the illegally-appointed incumbents of Harrow and of Throwley.

18. Ranulf de Broc had seized a cargo of wine which was on its way to Thomas from France, with clearance from the king, and had killed some of the sailors and imprisoned others at Pevensey. Orders for redress had been obtained from the Young King. *Materials*, III, 124.

19. FitzStephen makes it clear that these contradictory orders were given in quick succession—FitzUrse told the crowd to stand back, then, seeing that they were not going to do so, at once ordered them to keep the Archbishop securely. *Materials*, III, 135.

20. Vespers was sung twice daily in the cathedral, by the monks, and by the Archbishop's clerks. This was the monks' vespers that was now going on.

21. The author of the *Life of Saint Thomas* so often referred to. He was an Englishman, born at Cambridge, and was in Canterbury visiting the Archbishop.

22. Alexander Llewllyn, Thomas's crossbearer, one of his most faithful companions. Herbert of Bosham calls him *jocundus in verbis et in verbis jocundis multus*. (*Materials*, III, 528). He was not present at the murder, as Thomas had sent him and Herbert to France with messages two days before.

23. Archbishop of Canterbury 1006-1012, murdered by Danes.

24. According to other versions, he walked along with dignity, the last of the procession.

25. 'Bolt' translates *loc* (which translates *sera*); it may have been any kind of latch or fastening.

26. Hugh of Horsea. Mauclerc ('Ill-clerk') was a common surname, implying nothing worse than lack of scholarship. Cf. Beauclerc, one who was literate.

27. These knights did not exist and owe their presence here to Garnier's misunderstanding of his original. See Walberg, p. xlii.

28. i.e., the steps that were almost opposite the door in from the cloister, and led up to the north aisle. There were also stairs going up to the right, which led under the central tower and so into the choir. (It is all quite different now.)

29. Also it would have been dark inside the cathedral, at about five o'clock on a midwinter evening.

30. Garnier seems to be working on the principle that if he includes all the alternatives offered by his sources, some of it is bound to be right.

31. Garnier's variations on the meanings of the words 'pillar' and 'head' are in the true medieval rhetorical tradition. His likening of Thomas to Christ is typical of the attitude of all the biographers—Herbert refers to himself as 'the disciple that wrote these things'. The passage about 'the head's head' means something like: the (physical) head of the head (of the church—the archbishop) had to be sacrificed for the sake of the wellbeing, strength, freedom, of the church. I am indebted to Professor M. D. Legge for help here.

32. William de Tracy.

33. The place in the north transept where Thomas was killed.

34. Henry II; another reference to his forest laws.

35. 'Blade' translates *cultel*, which may be any kind of knife, dagger or sword.

36. The text reads *E del pueple e des jurs fu la disme salvee*, on which Walberg comments 'Je ne saisis pas bien le sens exact de ce vers'. Dr. A. B. Emden, however, suggests that Garnier is using the word *disme*, 'tenth', in two senses, and that the line therefore means that '10 days' out of the year were saved, and so was 'the tithe' the people would have had to pay for reconsecration if the church had lain desecrated for a whole year. The reconsecration was performed on 21 December by the bishops of Exeter and of Chester.

37. King Henry, Duke of Normandy.

38. It was a matter of regret later to the brethren at Canterbury that they had parted so thoughtlessly with what turned out to be valuable relics.

39. 'Brabançons' meant any kind of mercenary.

40. One wonders why the ancient Jews should have 'expected' (*quidierent*) to be exiled. The reference may be to the cry 'His blood be upon us and on our children', or to prophecies of the destruction of Jerusalem.

Chapter Ten

1. There is a strong tradition that the biblical St. Thomas took the gospel to India. The reference to the five steps is not immediately clear; no recorded Ladders of Perfection consist of this number of steps. One possibility is that Garnier had in mind the *Scala Dei Minor, seu de gradibus charitatis*, of Honorius of Autun, but had not remembered it correctly. This is a ladder composed of 15 virtues, not five; but one of the reasons Honorius puts forward for using the number 15 is that 'fifteen is three fives, and, through faith in the Holy Trinity, we are to perform the works of charity with our five senses'—exactly what Garnier has just said that the two St. Thomases did. Migne, *Patrologia*, clxxii, 1239.

2. This author calls himself both Guernes and Garnier (pages 156 and 163), these being respectively the nominative and oblique forms of his name. Walberg preferred to use 'Guernes', but otherwise he has more usually been known as 'Garnier'.

3. These *ampullae* were at first made of earthenware, then of lead, as being less breakable.

4. The lepers' hospital at Harbledown, three miles out of Canterbury on the London road, founded by Lanfranc, now a home for old people. Henry's grant to it of £13 6s. 8d. a year is recorded in the Pipe Rolls for 1174-5, pp. 208, 213, and in those of subsequent years. It is still paid; see Urry, 'Two notes on Guernes de Pont Saint-Maxence' in *Archaeologia Cantiana*, lxvi, 96-7.

5. The Pipe Rolls just cited record such a payment 'to the hospital of Blean' (*Hospitali de Blien*). This hospital may perhaps be the one recorded in 1384 at Boughton under Blean, some four miles west of Harbledown (*V.C.H. Kent*, II, 208), but the identification is not certain, as the Blean was an extensive area, including Harbledown and several other villages.

6. Garnier's text does not make it clear whether blessing is invoked on Henry, directed by God to the hospital, or on whatever person it was that got Henry to go there; nor are we sure whether Henry or the hospital is to be improved. It reads: *Benei seit de Deu ki al liu le turna / Altrement qu'il n'en est e qui l'amendera.*

7. In the crypt, the western part of which is just as it was then.

8. His name appears to have been Walter; he was present at Thomas's funeral. Boxley was a Cistercian abbey near Maidstone, Kent. *V.C.H. Kent*, II. 155.

9. She was Rohesia; she died in 1184 or 1185 and her son John inherited this income. The other known sisters of St. Thomas are: Agnes, who founded a hospital on the site of their parents' house in Cheapside; and Mary, abbess of Barking, Essex.

10. Philippe, count of Flanders, was preparing to invade England in alliance with the Young King, but the king of France, hearing that Henry was in England, recalled him, and they went to beseige Rouen instead.

11. William the Lion, 1143-1214; defeated and captured 13 July as he was beseiging Alnwick.

12. He was a doctor in Canterbury, and physician to the monks; see Urry, 'The visions of Master Feramin', *39th Annual Report of the Friends of Canterbury Cathedral* (1966), and his *Canterbury under the Angevin Kings*, p. 166 and generally.

13. See Geoffrey of Monmouth's *History of the Kings of Britain*, tr. L. Thorpe (Penguins, 1966), pp. 170-185, for Merlin's prophecies; and see Walberg, pp. 314-5, for an attempt to interpret Garnier's interpretation.

14. Garnier takes *aquila rupti foederis*, the Eagle of the Broken Covenant, to refer to Henry's queen, Eleanor. She was arrested in March 1173 as an accomplice of her sons in revolt, and remained a prisoner till Henry died in 1189.

15. She had had two daughters by her first marriage with Louis VII, and eight children by Henry.

16. Margaret, daughter of Louis VII, married in infancy to Henry's son Henry. The king had her brought to England in July 1174, and she was kept under guard at Devizes till peace was settled.

Postscript

1. Thomas's sister Mary was made abbess of Barking, a post usually filled by the daughters of kings, in April 1173.

2. Prior 1167-1175; then abbot of Battle at Hastings; died 1199 or 1200.

INDEX